"As someone who is intimately familiar with the pain of loss, this is the hope-filled resource I wish I had during those dark days of grief. As I read Katrina's words, I felt seen, known, and held in my experience and ultimately ushered into the ever-present hope we have in Jesus. I know you will too. Thank you, Katrina, for this courageous offering."

NICOLE ZASOWSKI
marriage and family therapist;
author of *What If It's Wonderful?*

"Larson's daily entries are messy, real, and relatable, reminding us that we never grieve alone and that hope really does endure."

JASON HAGUE
associate pastor of Christ's Center Church, Oregon;
author of *Mid-Faith Crisis and Aching Joy*

Faith, Hope, *and* Love in a Time *of* Loss

A 90-Day Devotional through Grief

Faith, Hope, *and* Love in a Time *of* Loss

A 90-Day Devotional through Grief

Katrina Larson

LEXHAM PRESS

Faith, Hope, and Love in a Time of Loss: A 90-Day Devotional through Grief

Lexham Press, 1313 Bay St, Bellingham 98225
LexhamPress.com

A continuation of the copyright information for Scripture quotations can be found on page 263.

Print ISBN 9781683598459
Digital ISBN 9781683598442

Lexham Editorial: Abigail Stocker, Rachel Joy Welcher, Allisyn Ma, Mandi Newell
Cover Design: Gabriel Eason
Typesetting: Jessi Strong

25 26 27 28 29 30 31 / US / 12 11 10 9 8 7 6 5 4 3 2 1

CONTENTS

Part Two: Faith, Hope, Love

Part Three: The Greatest of These Is Love

AND NOW
these three remain:

faith,

hope,

and love.

BUT THE GREATEST
OF THESE
is

love.

1 CORINTHIANS 13:13

A Prayer for the Ones Who Remain Behind

When the casseroles have been reheated and the freezer is bare,
 you remain, O God.

When the lights go out in the carpeted halls,
 where we remembered our loved ones and cried,
 you are there.

When the tears create familiar trails down our cheeks,
 you are there.

When our limbs and hearts grow numb,
 not allowing us to feel anything at all, you are there.

When the gifts and cards stop and the flowers die, you are there.

When we bury our noses in the fibers of their old clothes,
 searching for the scent of their presence, you are there.

When our faith bows beneath the weight of our *whys*,
 you graft us into your tree of life.

When our hope that things will go back to "normal" fades,
 like early evening light, you give us a new future.

When our love for the one who died reverberates out for an answer,
 you call out our names.

What remains, God, in the ashes of our grief?

What remains, God, in the hollow echoes of loss?

Where could we go that you would not follow?

If we make our bed in darkness, with oceans of tears around us,
 you are there.

If we fly above the clouds and dance around with birds,
 you are there.

You remain.

PART 1

THESE THREE REMAIN

Faith, hope, and love
are characteristics of God we can see
in our past, present, and future lives
as grieving people.

DAY 1

FAITH IS THE FIRST STEP

They will be like a tree planted by the water that sends out its roots by the stream. It does not fear when heat comes; its leaves are always green. It has no worries in a year of drought and never fails to bear fruit. —Jeremiah 17:8 NIV

On a cold day in February, my sister and I drove three hours to our hometown to wait. We sat on plastic-cushioned chairs in the hospital lobby. My dad would soon exit the elevator with an update on my mom's diagnosis. The illness began quietly with a simple cough in her chest, then falling asleep earlier than normal, and finally, her left leg suddenly stopped working at random moments. When my dad sat beside us that day, he spoke softly, but the message was a loud and horrible noise: stage four lung cancer. Six months to live.

These moments are heavy.

Perhaps your own story of sorrow starts in a similar way. An unexpected diagnosis. A crushing loss. A goodbye you never wanted to say. A sudden breaking point that led to a giant chasm of pain.

My legs burned that day in the hospital lobby. I looked down at the sparkling blue engagement ring on my finger. I wanted to run away so badly—to run out of the lobby and straight toward my happy ending that I had always hoped for, dreamed for, and prayed for. I wanted to feel the sting of winter wind on my face and not the sterile air of St. Peter's Hospital. I wanted to flee from the news that my mom had only months to live. I needed decades with her.

Just a few weeks before this, I had stepped into the perfect white dress in a bridal store and twirled in front of the full-length mirror. All hope, and no grief. All promise, with no death. And my mom had jumped up and down beside me with happy tears. I wanted to run toward the fantasy of a perfect wedding as a beautiful bride with a supportive, healthy mother watching with joy spread across her face.

What keeps you grounded in moments like this? What reminds you to take small, sure steps even when you are scared and heartbroken? When we have faith, God reminds us that he promised never to leave us. Faith invites us to stay and be present because God doesn't run away. He sustains us even in times of drought.

I started my twenties at a sprint only to realize that life is a marathon that requires strength, perseverance, and lots of faith. Faith sustained me to reach beyond my own limitations and to find strength in Jesus so I could become a tree planted by streams of water with deep roots.

Even though I wanted to run away from that hospital lobby that day—run away from my grief, my family, and the hard things that would follow—I stayed, prompted by the Holy Spirit to take small steps toward my mom's hospital room. I climbed in the hospital bed beside her and, for a moment, we laughed together about silly things like we always had.

Dear Jesus, I want to run away from difficult news.

Please plant me like a tree by your river.

Grow my roots and my faith deep so that I might remain still and green during these devastating, life-altering moments.

Be my home when my own feels like it is crumbling around me.

Be my living water in times of drought. Amen.

DAY 2

HOPE IN THE BREAKING

And he took bread, and when he had given thanks, he broke it and gave it to them, saying, "This is my body, which is given for you. Do this in remembrance of me." —Luke 22:19 ESV

My dad stood in front of a conference room filled with fleece-clad government employees who spent most of their days working outside. A young coworker of theirs had died recently from a tragic and horrific machinery accident. *What should I share?* he thought, running hand through brown hair peppered with gray. My dad worked as a counselor for Washington state workers, and part of his job was to facilitate a safe space for people to process their grief when a crisis arose. The people before him were the ones who had spent their days tending to and protecting Washington State's natural resources, parks, and living things. Cascading waterfalls, vibrant rivers, and tender shoots of grass were all under their jurisdiction.

The nature of my dad's job meant that he could never volunteer too much information about his day to me, but if I saw headlines of a judge getting bomb threats, a ferry worker dying in a fall, or a suicide on a state college campus, I knew there was a good chance he was debriefing the government workers involved. He shared bits and pieces of this day with me, and I filled in the rest with my imagination.

"Our bodies are like walnuts falling from a tree," he told them. The words came slowly, thoughtfully. "When we die, the outer shell is broken." He brought his hands together and paused for a moment. "Death is a natural part of this life. And when our bodies fade, the interior part of our souls still endures." Like the seed inside the walnut is buried to start new growth, our souls remain and endure even after our bodies decay. It had been one year since he lost my mom, and he had spent time considering death from many angles. He had never been afraid to speak the truth at his job, but in the months following my mom's death, his speech became punctuated by bold wisdom. Soon after my dad finished his brief introduction, he opened up the floor for people to share their grief. When he began, this group sat still and quiet, like faded stones on a salty beach. After the metaphor of the walnut, however, each person started to open up like young leaves growing toward the sun. Healing could finally begin.

Death is a natural and expected part of life, like walnuts whose shells are created to crack in order to release a new seed of growth. I know that breaking open is inevitable. I've seen people I love die, but I know that death is not the end. Jesus stands before us and offers up his broken body, sacrificed on a beautiful tree that we twisted into a tool of death. He holds up a walnut—an ordinary brown color with soft, black veins running through its sides—and reminds us, "These three remain: faith, hope, and love. I remain." Jesus stands with us—a seed of hope planted within our souls. Even though we may break, he will endure. He reminds us that his hope is unbreakable.

Dear Jesus, thank you for never shrinking away from death and for becoming a human willing to be broken for us.

You said, "This is my body, which is given for you" as you broke apart the bread.

You know what it's like for me to exist in this fragile shell of my body.

Protect and comfort my soul as I remember that death is a part of this world.

Help me to be unafraid to talk about death with others. Amen.

DAY 3

LOVE CHEERS YOU ON

I have fought the good fight, I have finished the race, I have kept the faith. —2 Timothy 4:7 NIV

My brother crumpled with exhaustion as he crossed the finish line. My dad embraced him in a big hug as the harsh Montana wind cut across our faces. It was my brother's last cross-country race of his collegiate career. My dad, older sister, and I drove for twenty-four hours on roads with mountain views and past elk herds just to watch this race. The memory of my mom's love was like a heavy jacket that day that provided warmth for our hearts. We were being folded like origami paper into new shapes. We had crossed the first big milestone without her.

The following Christmas, my sister gifted my dad a framed black-and-white photo of this moment with my brother. My dad is smiling, and the weariness and relief is evident on my brother's lean face. It sits on top of my dad's upright piano, a snapshot of a proud father holding up his child.

God not only celebrates with us at each finish line; he runs beside us the whole time. At the end, he receives us with the words: "Well done, good and faithful servant!" (Matthew 25:23 NIV). Isaiah 40:30 tells us that "even youths will become weak and tired, and young men will fall in exhaustion" (NLT). Grief does not discriminate based upon age or abilities. Even the youngest and strongest among us fall under its weight. But God says that "those who trust in the LORD will find new strength" (Isaiah 40:31 NLT), and that is a promise for each one of us. Each day that we get up and choose to continue to love others and love God is a race well run. At the end of each day, we can collapse into the loving arms of our Father for he will always remain by our side.

Dear God, give me the strength and perseverance to get through today.

I trust in you.

Let the memory of my loved one be a comfort and an encouragement to continue in your love.

Cheer me on when I grow tired and need to persevere to the finish line.

One day, I know I will stand before you and
you will tell me that I have "fought the good fight,
I have finished the race, I have kept the faith."
Amen.

DAY 4

REMAIN BY GOD'S SIDE

We've been surrounded and battered by troubles, but we're not demoralized; we're not sure what to do, but we know that God knows what to do; we've been spiritually terrorized, but God hasn't left our side; we've been thrown down, but we haven't broken. —2 Corinthians 4:8b–9 MSG

I was struggling to get the whisk attachment out of the mixing bowl when my coworker hit me with the question I hoped no one would ask that day: "Are you going to see your mom this weekend?" We stood side by side in the galley kitchen, making whipped cream to top cheesecakes. Mother's Day was two days away, and all I wanted to do was bury myself under the covers, eat chocolate, and enjoy the movies my mom and I used to watch together.

My coworker had unwittingly stumbled upon a painful conversation topic for me. I took a deep breath and replied, "Actually, she passed away last summer. So, I'm having a low-key weekend at home." She immediately said how sorry she was and gave me a kind look. We moved on to safer topics of conversation and began dolloping large clumps of whipped cream into the center of the cheesecakes. As I smoothed my spatula from the center of the cake outward to create a perfect spiral, I was hit with the realization that my mom would have been so proud of me. I imagined her saying, "My little Trina, of course you're making cheesecakes. You always loved dessert!"

Making whipped cream takes time. You have to agitate the heavy cream in a mixer until it forms stiff peaks. Agitation and resistance are part of the process. When an everyday moment triggers grief, it can feel like we're stuck in a mixer. Grief can turn us around, leaving us disoriented and feeling small. Even though we can feel battered and surrounded by grief's waves, God remains there with us. He does not beat us down but builds us up through the process of refinement. He was churning my troubled soul into peaks of peace. I held my breath in the days leading up to each of those first anniversaries, holidays, and milestones without my mom. I steeled myself for the inevitable questions from well-meaning people. I was mixed up in grief, but God knew my troubles as folding me into his never-ending, faithful love.

Dear God, I don't always know what to do or say, but I know you are never uncomfortable or awkward with my grief.

Even though "we have been surrounded and battered by troubles; ... we're not sure what to do, but we know that God knows what to do" (2 Corinthians 4:9 MSG).

You do not beat me down but build me up.

I lean into your strength and love today. Amen.

DAY 5

REMAIN FULL OF GRACE AND JOY

And why do you worry about clothes? See how the flowers of the field grow. They do not labor or spin. Yet I tell you that not even Solomon in all his splendor was dressed like one of these.
—Matthew 6:28 NIV

My feet pounded the pavement and bright pink splotches colored my cheeks as I flushed with exertion. "Just one more hill!" My sister egged me on, running a few steps ahead of me. "Just one more hill until my face looks like a tomato," I thought to myself. The months my family and I spent taking care of my mom during her cancer were filled with lots of sitting—sitting beside my mom at doctor's appointments, sitting with her on the couch watching movies, and sitting on long car rides with my sister commuting back and forth to my parents' house. My physical health had been pushed to the side like a wildflower struggling for purchase by the highway. It felt physically and mentally painful to begin caring for my body again.

As I jogged into the driveway of my sister's house, breathing hard and sweating buckets, my husband, Jesse, came out of the front door and said, "Hey! You look so cute." I realized in that moment that I needed to extend the same grace and joy that Jesse extended to me to myself. There is no race toward healing, just small steps in the right direction. Will I ever have the same carefree spirit I used to, running unburdened and strong like I did before mom died? Maybe I will. Maybe I will not. Either way, it was time to start letting the weight of caring for my mother go.

I had carried the mental load of her sickness for the four months leading up to her death, and part of me was worried that if I took care of myself, it would mean she was really gone. God spoke to me as I began to walk and cool down that day. "Look at the daisies," he said, "how they are clothed in the finest dresses every day. Why are you so worried about yourself?" If even the humble roadside daisy is cared for by God, how much more so are we?

Dear God, you clothe the flowers of the field in the finest clothing and provide all that they need.

If you take so much care for temporary wildflowers, how much more must you care for me?

Help me take steps toward mentally and physically caring for myself again.

You always extend grace and joy toward me and take on my heavy burdens. Amen.

DAY 6

FAITH IN GOD'S DYNAMIC WORDS

But they delight in the law of the Lord,
meditating on it day and night. —Psalm 1:2 NLT

As a preschooler, I would often wake before the sun rose. My dad would look up from the couch and see me walking down the stairs in my Barbie pajamas. He would make me a cup of hot chocolate to match his mocha, and I would snuggle beside him while he balanced his Bible on his knees. He would meditate and pray as the sun rose through the living room windows. When I think of meditating on the law of the Lord day and night, I think of my parents and how, in the same way the sun rises in the morning and the moon appears at night, they bookended each day with God's words. They were not perfect people, but they showed me how God's word could become a part of our imperfect lives. I was always watching them, soaking in their example and presence.

Every Tuesday night, for over ten years, my mom helped lead the women's Bible study at our local church. As the light faded in the windows of the fellowship hall and stale decaf coffee was served in carafes, my mom would make PowerPoint slides come alive with her faith and conviction in God's word. Her voice echoed across the folding chairs, and her brown eyes met the eyes of each woman in the crowd. She didn't only teach them, she showed up for them when they were in the hospital, took care of their babies, and prayed over their victories and losses. I watched as each of those same ladies showed up at my mother's door with casseroles, pies, and kind eyes when she was sick.

I don't want to get to the end of my life and realize I read a bunch of Bible verses but didn't show up at my friend's hospital bedside or that I didn't bring them a meal when they were too weak to cook. I want faith, hope, and love to be evident through the things I say and the actions I choose. Spending time reading, thinking, and talking about God's word should motivate us to be present with others. Just like a child observes and soaks up their parents' example, we become more intimately acquainted with God when we spend time in his presence. And his presence is our delight.

Dear Jesus, you have promised and you are faithful.

Your word is living, active, and sharper
than any sword (Hebrews 4:12).

I can sit in your presence and soak in your wisdom.

Remind me of your words all throughout
the day and the night.

Bring people into my life who delight in your word
and can be spiritual parents to me. Amen.

DAY 7

HOPE IN A GOD WHO MADE THE STARS

Lift up your eyes and look to the heavens: Who created all these? He who brings out the starry host one by one and calls forth each of them by name. Because of his great power and mighty strength, not one of them is missing.

—Isaiah 40:26 NIV

In December, shortly after my mom died, Jesse and I found ourselves underneath a giant ornamented tree in the middle of an outdoor shopping center. Our stomachs were warm with spicy Thai food, and our cheeks were pink from the cold. The Christmas lights glowed faintly around the tree, which paled in comparison to the light show happening above us in the sky. I watched people walk by, bundled up in scarves as the moon lit up the surrounding shops. That night, I wondered about the star that led people to Christ years ago. What did it look like? Where did it first appear?

I wondered if it lit the world up the way headlights light a dark highway in the middle of a storm. Or like a lighthouse, burning brightly, leading ships home. I also wondered if it remained a mystery to most people, only truly recognized by the wisemen or others with their heads tilted toward the sky. But underneath all of this wondering about that special Christmas star remained an even bigger question: Did the God who created each and every star care about me? Could I place my hope in him this cold December? Would he recognize my grieving heart burning dimly underneath all these artificially colored lights?

My knowledge of stars is limited to an Astronomy 101 course I took in college, but I still remember learning that when we look at stars, we are looking at pictures of the past. By the time the light reaches us, the star may be dying or a completely new one may have formed. Grief can be the same way, especially during the holidays. We're looking at memories from the past, sometimes so consumed that we are unaware of what's happening in the present. But God cares about grievers because he is the creator of all. The Bible says that God counts every star and knows them by name. If he keeps track of every star in the sky, how much more will he know and take care of us—his children?

God knows your future, and he knows your past. He knows when you miss someone dearly, and he knows when family and holidays are hard. But his hope burns brighter than any star. Even when we cannot see it, he has called us by name underneath an inky sky.

Dear Jesus, help me to look up and see the signs of
hope you have provided for me.

Because of your great power and mighty strength,
you keep track of every single star,
and I know you see and care for me too.

Thank you for being a gentle and gracious God. Amen.

DAY 8

LOVE WILL REMAIN

For now we see only a reflection as in a mirror; then we shall see face to face. Now I know in part; then I shall know fully, even as I am fully known. —1 Corinthians 13:12 NIV

Bon Iver's falsetto played in the background as the few remaining customers strolled out the front door and the late-night rush came to a close. A half-finished, frothy latte sat on the counter before me, and the scent of toasted coconut wafted from the back kitchen. How did I end up here, working as a dessert shop employee, when my goal for the past four years had been to be a teacher? "Why am I here, God?" I silently asked myself as I tightened the apron around my waist. The shop was still warm from the crowd earlier. Their presence served as a welcome reprieve from my grief, which seemed to wait for me at home. I looked forward to every cake-filled shift, but in these quiet moments, at the end of the night, I had so many questions for God.

During a lull at the dessert shop that night, a verse came to my mind, seemingly unbidden, from the sweet air around me: "Now these three remain: faith, hope, and love" (1 Corinthians 13:13 NIV). Wasn't that the Bible verse I had loved before? Before mom died? Anxious to get moving, I grabbed the bottle of glass cleaner and a microfiber cloth and began to carefully wipe down the antique mirrors that decorated the lobby. As I brought the yellow cloth down the mirror, I caught my face in the reflection, and for a moment, I saw her. My mom. Her round eyes and fine, brown hair. I took a deep breath as I realized that her love endured not only in my features, which carried her DNA, but would also endure through my life going forward.

As I buffed out the streaks of dirt on the bottom of the glass, a glimpse of who God is was revealed to me. I was so much more than someone counting down the hours until I could go home and cry. It didn't matter *why* I was here, cleaning mirrors in a dessert shop, it mattered *who* was with me. First Corinthians 13:13 had been my treasured verse for three years before my mom got sick, and it returned to me now like an old friend. I needed God's incredible compassion to sustain me. I needed his love to be the reflection staring back at me. His love was all that remained.

Dear Jesus, you are with me always, just like the love I carry in my heart for those whom I've lost.

They are gone, but you will always be with me.

Your love remains in my life as my grief reveals itself more and more. Amen.

DAY 9

REMAIN IN HIS SPIRIT

Then he replied to me, "This is this message from the Lord *to Zerubbabel: 'Not by valor nor by strength, but only by my Spirit,' says the* Lord *of the Heavenly Armies."* —Zechariah 4:6 ISV

I signed up for piano lessons for the first time," Shirley said to me, her whole face lighting up with joy, making her blue eyes pop. Shirley had been friends with my mom since before I was born, and she and her husband were like a second set of parents to me. "That's wonderful!" I told her. Shirley explained that her dad had recently died, and she was ready to make a new tune out of her grief and try something she had never done before.

She pulled me into a hug and said to me, "It's all because of your blog post! You inspired me." I didn't know what to say for several moments. Shirley learned something from me? From the rubble of my grief? Only the Holy Spirit could take a simple blog post and have it speak exactly what a friend needs to hear. On the car ride home, I cried a few hot tears of thankfulness mixed with bittersweetness. I pictured Shirley sitting down at the piano, plunking out a song, and I wanted to tell my mom about it.

This moment reminded me of Zerubbabel's story in the Bible. Zerubbabel's name means "a stranger at Babylon."[1] He and his people had experienced the destruction of their temple by the Babylonians and had lived their lives as enemy captives far from home. The Lord gave Zerubbabel the job of rebuilding the temple when they were allowed to return. I imagine him standing in front of those dusty ruins, with large boulders of the broken temple scattered around him, the hot sun beating down on his back, and his eyes scanning the horizon for enemies. God told Zerubbabel that he would not accomplish this huge task using his own strength or valor but only with the help of God's Spirit.

Even when we are neck-deep in the ruins of grief, God meets us there to help us rebuild. Healing will not be accomplished through our own valor or strength, but only by his Spirit working in our hearts and through other people, like Shirley did for me. By the Holy Spirit's strength, we will accomplish the seemingly impossible task of moving forward.

Dear Jesus, give me strength and valor so that
I remember who I am in you.

I am a child of the king, and that's more important
than anything else.

You know exactly what I need to hear today,
and by your power I will step forward in faith.

Who you say I am remains beyond anything I feel
or experience. Amen.

---

1. Hitchcock's Bible Names Dictionary, "Zerubbabel," https://www.biblestudytools.com/dictionaries/hitchcocks-bible-names/zerubbabel.html.

DAY 10

REMAIN GENTLE TOWARD YOURSELF

Anyone who listens to my teaching and follows it is wise, like a person who builds a house on solid rock. Though the rain comes in torrents and the floodwaters rise and the winds beat against that house, it won't collapse because it is built on bedrock.

—Matthew 7:24–25 NLT

One day, I tearfully confessed to my husband, "I'm just not doing anything!" It felt like my days as a grieving person were lined up like dominoes, ready to collapse with a single push. Gone was the feeling of stability and productivity I had about my life before grief entered. He wisely patted me on the back and reminded me, "Be kind to yourself. You are a child of God." I think the Holy Spirit gave my husband the words I needed to hear in that moment. Maybe you need to hear them today too.

When I lost my mom, it felt like a part of my identity was ripped from me. I was no longer a daughter to a mother alive on this earth. My identity was stripped down to the essentials: faith, hope, and love. Faith to keep following God even as all my assumptions were crashing down around me. Hope that God would help me figure out what my life would be like without her. And love to remind me that God loved me because I was his child, no matter what I lost or gained. In the span of one year, I had graduated college, worked as an AmeriCorps volunteer, married Jesse, and then my mom died. The identities and titles I had held so dearly were all of sudden taken away and replaced with new ones I didn't understand.

Grief is a huge transition—one that is ripe with the opportunity to practice gentleness, patience, and persistent grace toward yourself. Rather than seeing this time as a bunch of dominoes ready to fall at any moment, you are a house built on a firm foundation that cannot fall. That doesn't mean you won't feel the wind beating against your back or watch the floodwaters rise around your house. It means that God is your center, your foundation, and your ultimate identity. No matter how your life changes, or how the seemingly endless days of grief stretch on, he does not change. He loves us apart from what we accomplish.

The grief process is not linear. Grief looks (and feels) more like a roller coaster: dizzying heights, swift descents, and loop the loops that literally turn your world upside down. It's no wonder that our emotions and thoughts about ourselves vary so widely in our grief. But we can observe these patterns of grief without allowing them to become our identity. The Father has given us the kind of wonderful, overflowing love that secures us in his family. This love operates apart from the roller coaster of grief.

Your identity in Christ isn't dependent upon what you do for him or what the grief process looks like for you. Instead of trying to fight off unkind thoughts toward yourself, try sitting with them for a moment. Observe them like you would watch a roller coaster ride at a theme park. You might say to yourself, "Huh, that's interesting," or, "Look at that unexpected turn." It doesn't really matter what you say as long as you try to approach these moments as an observer instead of as a fixer. I like to imagine I am sitting on a bench watching the ride as Jesus sits next to me.

During the early days of grief, I often said to myself, "I'm just not doing anything!" And I suppose that was true, at least, according to the world's standards and my own expectations. But what I was not noticing, and what could not be seen on the outside, was the inner work I was doing. Observing my grief and letting Jesus enter into that space with me was no small task. In fact, it was incredibly difficult at times. But through my time with him, I have found my true identity as one of his children. He sees me just as I am; he loves me just as I am; and he will always remain.

Dear God, don't be far from me today.

I choose to build the foundation of my life upon your faith, hope, and love because I know you help me withstand the storms of my grief.

Let me know you more in this season.

Help me to be kind and gentle toward myself because you are kind and gentle to me. Amen.

DAY 11

FAITH IS A TREE PLANTED BY WATER

They are like trees planted along the riverbank, bearing fruit each season. Their leaves never wither, and they prosper in all they do.
—Psalm 1:3 NLT

Growing up, there was a maple tree in the yard. Its limbs spread like an umbrella over the grass, and the woods behind it stretched for over a mile. One time, my siblings and I found an abandoned Volkswagen Bug in those woods and fabricated a story where it was a getaway car for a robbery. The trunks of the trees around it were scarred, and we learned later that a forest fire had probably razed the trees, which allowed room for regrowth. We lived and breathed the tree and the forest behind it. In the fall, this majestic maple tree left behind its leaves, and on Thanksgiving weekend, we would rake them up with the promise of my mom's holiday leftovers after our hard work. In the winter, I would watch the snow drip from its branches as I sat on the back of the couch. In the spring, my dad would mow the lawn around it, and a deer would hide behind it, usually with twin fawns following close by. In the summer, we would build a firepit and put up a tent beneath its leafy green canopy.

A year before my mom died, we returned to our childhood home to find the entire forest chopped down. All that was left was a thin line of trees bordering our one-acre property. The lot behind ours had just been sold to a new owner, a new family. This was not the natural regrowth process of a forest fire.

But there stood the maple tree, safe behind the property line. The same, but different. In college, my mentor told me to be like a tree—the kind of person other people could find and seek refuge under. One of the people I tried to shelter was my friend Haley. She always carried sketchbooks and big questions, and she struggled with her mental health and trauma from her past. As her small group leader, I tried to support her in finding answers.

In the spring of my sophomore year at college, Haley's trauma sparked a dangerous flame that took over her life like a large forest fire blazing through. This fire culminated with her facing demons I couldn't fight for her. The rest is her story to tell, but my heart was deeply grieved for Haley, and I partially blamed myself for her trauma coming to a head. I found no shade or solace to give her.

My walk to campus wove through an arboretum, which was filled with lush trees, winding paths, and dense foliage. It smelled like sweet sticky pine needles and rotting leaves. On my walks, I would talk to God and shake my hands in frustration. "What are you doing?" I would ask. "And why did you allow these things to happen?" Oftentimes, my only answer was the wind blowing through the trees.

Our last small group of the year, we had a picnic at a waterfront park on a small pebbly beach. We spread a blanket over the rocks and had sparkling apple juice and strawberries. Thankfully, Haley was getting the help she needed and was now stable. My mentor's words came back to me at that moment: "Be like a tree." A tree takes in the elements (rain, wind, scorching sun) and bears fruit. A tree has roots that make it unshakable. I looked up and saw a tree on the banks of the beach, its branches growing wide and tall, and its leaves reaching for the sunset's last bit of warmth. The tree provided soft shade for our little group on the beach that day.

Haley and the ladies around me did not need me to provide answers, or to solve their complex hurts. They needed a friend to listen, to sit under a tree with them, and enjoy the fruits provided. They needed someone faithful with roots connected to the faithfulness of Jesus.

Lord, help me to be a tree planted by water
with roots growing strong in your living
faithfulness, sustained and nurtured
by your presence.

I don't need to prove anything to you.

I just need to embrace your faithfulness
and let it spring forth from my life. Amen.

DAY 12

HOPE NEVER LEAVES US

Keep on asking, and you will receive what you ask for. Keep on seeking, and you will find. Keep on knocking, and the door will be opened to you. —Matthew 7:7 NLT

It was midafternoon on a bright fall Sunday when my life changed forever. (Well, not right away, but it was definitely the beginning.) It was my first week as a building supervisor for the recreation center on campus at my university. I tugged on my red polo nervously as I swiped students' ID cards and made sure my fellow employees showed up for their shifts. The gym was fairly busy that weekend since students were still motivated to work out while their class loads were still relatively light. I watched as a steady stream of students made their way through the turnstiles.

Then, there he was: Jesse Larson. Six feet tall. Thick-rimmed glasses. Tanned face from time spent at home in southern California. I recognized him from mutual friends we had from the Christian group on campus, and my heart skipped a beat. My position of authority temporarily gave me courage (as well as the thick desk between us), and I said, "Hey! I think we have friends in common. It's Jesse, right?" He replied, "Yep, that's me," and he handed me a card that clearly read "Chris Brown." I felt trapped between maintaining my new professional role and offending someone I liked. I told him, "I'm sorry, this isn't your ID card. I can't let you in." I was supposed to confiscate the card and have him get in trouble with my supervisor, but instead, I gave it back to him. Jesse was confused and said, "Are you serious?" with an exasperated look on his face. I didn't back down, and he walked out. As I watched him leave the building, my shoulders sank.

We got married two and a half years later.

It was early one evening on a drizzly Friday in April when we exchanged vows. The same exasperated guy with the borrowed ID turned out to be one of the most persistent and kind people I had ever met. God knew I needed someone who would back me up when I told my family and friends we were moving up our wedding by three months. Someone who wouldn't run away or be intimidated by joining a family in the middle of their biggest tragedy. Someone not intimidated by a woman who stands her ground.

Jesse's dad performed our wedding ceremony and shared our story, including our infamous recreation center meeting. I realized as I stood in my wedding dress, looking at Jesse, that neither of us was the same person as that day we first met. I was no longer trapped between asserting my own identity and pleasing other people. My mom's sickness, Jesse's and my relationship, and my own personal growth with God had shaped me into a braver, kinder, and wiser person. I knew that, as our marriage continued, we would both change again and again. But one thing had stayed the same: I still held to my convictions strongly and was not easily swayed. I didn't give up on Jesse, and he didn't give up on me.

Our wedding day ended in a dance party. Under twinkly lights and paper lanterns, my friends danced to "Uptown Funk" until they were sweaty and grinning. My mom got up and danced her last dance with my dad supporting her. I couldn't see it then, but I see it now. God never gives up on us. When we ask to draw near to him, he always opens the door wide to let us in. He is kind. He is persistent. He is not intimidated by our greatest tragedies and biggest insecurities. He shows up at our first awkward dance and supports us in the slow dances at the end of our lives. He never changes, and he never leaves us.

Dear God, you never change.

No matter how much I change or what I go through,
you are kind, persistent, and faithful.

You take the awkwardness of my grief and love me
through it all. Amen.

DAY 13

WHEN LOVE REQUIRES GRIT

Love never ends. As for prophecies, they will pass away; as for tongues, they will cease; as for knowledge, it will pass away.
—1 Corinthians 13:8 ESV

I was sitting on a sunny patch of grass when I received the phone call that my mom was in her last days. "You should come home, Trina," my aunt told me when I answered the phone. Looking out at the San Juan Islands and the crystal waters of the Samish Bay below me, and all I could think was "How can the view before me be so beautiful when I'm so devastated inside?" My year could be summed up by this moment. A time that was supposed to be ripe with opportunity and celebrations had instead been met with canceled plans, tough conversations, and solemn goodbyes. Jesse was supposed to graduate in five days; his family had plane tickets to come visit and watch the ceremony. We had been married for two months and were house-sitting for family friends until we found a place to rent. Everything we owned could fit into the trunk of my car. Instead of celebrating his graduation that weekend, we loaded up our bags and headed south. My aunt's words, "You should come home," echoed in my head every mile we drove. The next time I saw Jesse's family was at my mom's memorial service three weeks later. Just like that, mom was gone.

"What now, God?" I remember thinking to myself in the weeks after my mom's memorial. My sister sagely said to me, "I'm not going to give up on God just because my mom died." I loved how boldly she explained it. We come from a long line of strong women who needed grit and love to make it through. My grandma had six kids by the time she was twenty six and raised them with limited means on a small farm in Onalaska, Washington. My mom, like her mother, carried that farm girl ethic throughout her life and dug her heels in when times were hard. But there was always a softness to her when you were hurt or needed to talk. After she died, I faced a strange combination of feelings—a blend of sorrow and celebration. As newlyweds, Jesse and I were beginning to form our own family. I was also grieving the loss of the matriarch and anchor for the family I had come from. How could I embark on the next chapter of my life without my mom to help me transition?

In those days, I clung to the things that do not pass away, like the love and grit my grandma, mom, and sister had shown me. The times I doubted my faith, because of my pain, I remembered they didn't give up. The women in my family didn't give up because they knew that God is with us across the entirety of our lives—from the greatest celebrations to the most devastating phone calls. The beautiful views of life are sometimes accompanied by dark and difficult feelings. Life can be messy, and that scares us sometimes. We want life and emotions to be organized in neat boxes, but that's not how it goes. Having our lives figured out is not a requirement for approaching God with our questions and feelings. He takes our stubborn persistence and helps soften it into loving grace for ourselves and others. One thing that does not pass away is the love of God. We should not give up on God because he's never going to give up on us.

Dear God, help me to continue showing grit and love
when things are really difficult.

Teach me to rely on your love
in moments that feel dark.

Just like a mother's love for her children,
your love never ends. Amen.

DAY 14

GRIEVING IN A DESSERT SHOP

He replied, "You must love the Lord your God with all your heart, with all your being, and with all your mind. This is the first and greatest commandment. And the second is like it: You must love your neighbor as you love yourself."
—Matthew 22:37–39 CEB

One morning, as I got ready for my shift at the dessert shop, I realized that I was the strongest and healthiest that I had been since my mom died. This realization made me cry messy tears because life was still really hard. I thought if I could just find a way to make the good days outnumber the bad days, I would be fine. If I faced my grief instead of running from it, I would be OK. I had a "plan" for how to manage my grief, but there was just one thing missing.

I kept thinking, "I wish I could tell her how I'm doing," and I couldn't. My mom was my go-to person to call if I didn't know to defrost raw chicken, had a bad day at work, or just wanted to chat. Just as we had begun that next chapter in our relationship, exploring how to be friends now that I was an adult, she died. It felt like I turned the page only to read, "To be continued ..." And I knew it was going to be a long time before that story was finished, and it wasn't going to be answered here on earth.

Near the end of my shift at the dessert shop that day, two of my favorite customers came in. They were a mom and daughter pair who visited the shop every Monday night and ordered a sugar cookie and a cupcake to share together on the big fluffy pink couch underneath the velvet pink curtains of the shop's front window. Even though it pained me to see their love, it also made my heart swell with happiness. They understood something so important that too many of us only realize in the wake of loss: time together is precious. It's the ritual of a Monday night. It's spending quality and a large quantity of time together, getting as much of both as you can. It's constantly choosing to be together over and over, so that when time runs out, you have those memories to hold close to your heart.

About two years before she died, my mom, dad, and brother were involved in a car accident on a rainy day on the freeway. I remember seeing my brother in a hospital bed, recovering from minor injuries, and noticing that my mother stood beside him wearing only one earring. My whole body felt numb with anger that they were left vulnerable like this, yet I was also relieved that the outcome hadn't been worse. In the following years, I made sure to give each of my family members a hug and to say, "I love you," any time we said goodbye. In some ways, I'm grateful that the car crash happened because it woke me up to how precious and fragile life is. I savored the time with my family those last two years, not fully understanding what would come next. I was given divine homework—to cherish time with those I love.

Daily seeing people share their love and bless one another helped me grieve. I saw friends meeting for coffee and cake. I saw families lighting birthday candles, their faces lit up by the glow. I put together a box of sugar cookies for a lady who had just received the call that she had terminal breast cancer. The pink curtains of the front window seemed to be pulled back on a regular basis in that shop, allowing me for a moment to see a glimpse into heaven. A cupcake can't really fix anything, but the kindness and the joy surrounding it reminded me that darkness can be fought. If we love the Lord Jesus with all our hearts, all our minds, and all our being, we can then love our neighbors, our family, our friends. The darkness can be pushed back, like a curtain, and we can see Jesus at the center of our celebrations and sorrows.

Dear Father, I sit in your presence today
and ask for guidance in my divine homework
to love others and you.

The hurt, the ache, and the "I wish I could tell them"
moments are hard.

Let your love shine through me to those around me
even in the darkness. Amen.

DAY 15

WHEN YOU'RE NOT ALRIGHT

Three times I pleaded with the Lord to take it away from me. But He said to me, "My grace is sufficient for you, for My power is made perfect in weakness." Therefore I will boast all the more gladly in my weaknesses, so that the power of Christ may rest on me. —2 Corinthians 12:8–9 BSB

I visited my in-laws' church in southern California the first Thanksgiving holiday weekend after my mom died. The teaching pastor talked about filling in the blanks in this phrase: "I'm not _____, but God is _____." The answer to the first blank came to me right away: I'm not alright. I was still wrestling with who God was in the wake of my fresh grief, and I struggled to fill in the second blank. But as soon as I admitted that I wasn't doing great, I felt relieved. The question had been running around in my brain for weeks: "What do I tell people when they ask how

I'm doing?" And the wholly inaccurate answer had been: "I'm alright." But I wasn't. I wasn't alright.

Our desire to prove that we can come out of the dark tunnel of grief is an exhausting goal. Fighting to prove something that isn't true is like holding your breath and making a wish as you pass through a tunnel, only to forget to breathe again as you enter back into the light. Being honest about how we are *really* doing is one way through that dark tunnel of initial grief. When I was finally honest with myself and God about how I was really doing, I finally found space to fill in that second blank: I'm not alright, but God is present.

As I rode through the winding mountain roads of the San Bernardino National Forest, heading to my in-laws' Lake Arrowhead cabin for Thanksgiving, I couldn't help but take in the vistas and reflect on the high highs and low lows of the past five months without my mom. As I watched the dizzying heights below, lit by the waning sun, I began to breathe more deeply. My mind was fresh with clearer air now that I had accepted how much I needed God and that I didn't have to prove anything to him or anyone else.

As we pulled into the cabin, it began to snow in great big flurries. The snow seemed to cleanse me of my earlier doubts as I watched my husband and brother-in-law toss a football in between unloading the truck. I was about to enter a room full of extended family I had only briefly met at our wedding. They all knew my mom had died, but I didn't know them at all. Early the next morning over fluffy scrambled eggs, Jesse's great aunt pulled me aside and said, "I'm so sorry to hear about your mom," and I said, "Thanks, I miss her a lot." That's all I had to say because being honest with myself and God made me not feel like I had to prove anything. I wasn't alright, but God was present.

Dear God, thank you for being so good
and true all the time.

I don't have to prove myself to you or anyone else
because you know how I am really doing.

You give me the right words to say at the right time.

Help me to be honest with you and others
in a way that allows room for healing.

I'm not alright, but you tell me, "My grace is sufficient
for you, for my power is made perfect in weakness."
Amen.

DAY 16

FAITH AND FRIENDS WHO BRING YOU TACOS

There are "friends" who destroy each other, but a real friend sticks closer than a brother. —Proverbs 18:24 NLT

"You're handling this so well! You're not even crying yourself to sleep anymore," my roommate said to me as we were brushing our teeth side by side a month after my mom was diagnosed with terminal lung cancer.

"I am still crying myself to sleep every night," I blurted out, toothbrush in hand.

Grieving can be so awkward at times. We put on a brave face when we need to, but sometimes we just need to admit to those we trust that we don't have it all together.

My roommate quickly apologized as I wiped the toothpaste from the corners of my mouth, and we both burst into an irrational giggle fit at the absurdity of it all. Here's the thing: your friends are going to say the wrong things. You are going to say the wrong things. So maybe it's time we shifted away from focusing on the words and paid more attention to our actions.

Specifically, to making tacos ... or whatever concrete, tangible ways we like to show love to one another. Five months later, my mom was gone and that same friend showed up at the door of our tiny home with tacos. She told me, "I don't know what to do, but I know how to make tacos." She had individually labeled each plastic container of sour cream, guacamole, salsa, and brought every topping imaginable.

Those tacos strengthened my bones (or maybe just my stomach, but they were delicious). They were like manna in a dry land of ramen packets. Tell your friends what specific, tangible needs they can help out with: gift cards, your favorite smoothie, movie theater tickets, time together with no agenda. Whatever feeds and nourishes your stomach and soul.

Jesus takes our humble gifts to each other and multiplies the blessings from them. In the Bible, a young boy gives up his meager meal of five loaves of bread and two fish, and Jesus turns it into a feast for over five thousand people. Why can't God take the small offerings of our friends and multiply the encouragement we receive from each? When you are honest with your friends and ask for help, you're inviting them into the miracle of a God who provides for our needs in tangible ways. Tell your friends that it is OK if they don't know what to do or say to someone who is grieving. Tell them to bring tacos anyway.

Dear Jesus, you always speak to us with truth and in love.

You lead us with lovingkindness.

You care about every part of us—our physical,
spiritual, and emotional needs.

Bring real friends into my life who can stick closer
than a brother.

You made us to be relational people
who care for each other.

Thank you for your grace and provision.

You alone can satisfy our every need,
and we place our faith in you. Amen.

DAY 17

HOPE IN THE GRACE OF GOD

This hope is like a firm and steady anchor for our souls. In fact, hope reaches behind the curtain and into the most holy place.
—Hebrews 6:19 CEV

Abide with me; fast falls the eventide;
The darkness deepens; Lord with me abide.
When other helpers fail and comforts flee,
Help of the helpless, O abide with me.
—"Abide with Me" by Henry Francis Lyte

I just want to die and be in heaven with mom," I thought to myself, lying on my bed, staring at the crack on the ceiling.[2] "Where did that come from?" I thought soon after. My cheeks turned red, and I felt shame flood my body. I didn't *actually* want

2. If you or someone you know is thinking about suicide, please call the suicide hotline at 988. You are a precious child of God and are loved abundantly.

to die, and I wasn't in any actual danger of harming myself. I just felt like my whole body was a sailboat without an anchor, pointing toward the horizon of heaven. Deep within my spirit was a longing to be where my mom was, and I felt burdened with the heaviness of this thought. I opened up a book about grief that a friend had given me. The chapter I read talked about how longing to be reunited with your loved one was a common feeling for grieving people. Relief flooded through me as I realized I wasn't alone.

Hope can feel like it is in short supply in those early days of grieving. What is there to look forward to? What is the future going to look like from now on? Who will be there to help me raise my kids someday? My questions as I laid in bed at night seemed to outweigh any thoughts I had about the future. My tender heart longed for heaven in the months following my mother's death. I realized that I needed to talk to my therapist about my feelings and not ignore or downplay them. Even though I wasn't alone in feeling this way, I needed to take the next step and get help processing these thoughts.

In those dark hours, staring at the ceiling, I became acquainted with grace. If hope was the anchor steadying me, grace was warmth of the first light of morning. After the storms of the night, where I felt like I was drowning in grief, grace reminded me I was loved abundantly by God. Paul describes it well when he says, "The grace of our Lord was poured out on me abundantly, along with the faith and love that are in Christ Jesus" (1 Timothy 1:14 NIV). Grace met me in the darkness of my thoughts, and instead of erasing or covering up my shame, it gave me the strength to not hide from God. Wanting to be in heaven with my mom was a reminder of my deep need to be reunited with God.

The beautiful thing about heaven is that we already have access to our heavenly Father, here and now. We don't have to wait to get to know him until we die. Paul says that God gave us the Holy Spirit as a down payment for our true home someday in heaven. Paul also says, "While we are living in the body, we are away from our home with the Lord" (2 Corinthians 5:6 CEB). When Jesus left this earth, he didn't leave us alone; he left his Holy Spirit to guide us as we navigate the tension between this earth and our true home with God in heaven.

In the wake of my mom's death, I struggled to balance the tension of longing for heaven while letting the Holy Spirit give me hope for the day ahead. I decided that, every time I had the thought, "I just want to die," I would also say to myself, "I just want to fly to Jesus." I would close my eyes and picture myself resting on his wings of mercy, reminding me to let his Spirit bear my burdens. His gift of mercy does not erase my desire to be reunited with my loved ones; in fact, it increases it all the more. God is my true home, and I long to be with him. At the end of time, he will set everything and everyone in right relationship with each other again. We can hope for eternity in its full glory as we live out the tension of a grace that has already been given to us.

Dear Lord, help me to accept the grace
you have so abundantly poured over me.

I miss my loved one so much,
and I wish I could be with them.

I long and hope for heaven while acknowledging
that your Holy Spirit is here with me now.

Anchor my soul in your real and present love. Amen.

DAY 18

LOVE SAYS YES AND AMEN

Christ says "Yes" to all God's promises. This is why we have Christ to say "Amen" for us to the glory of God.
—2 Corinthians 1:20 CEV

One cold January morning, Jesse showed up at my door with a bouquet of blue and white flowers and asked if I would go to a park with him. Once there, he pulled out a small blue journal with entries for every major milestone of our dating life and paused to read excerpts as we walked along the dirt path and stone bridges. All of this was leading to something ... and I had a pretty good idea what it was.

We arrived at a small clearing underneath the trees next to a waterfall. The river flowing from the waterfall roared below us, and a friend was hidden in the bushes ready to take pictures. Jesse played me a special song he had written and then got down on one knee and asked me to marry him. I said "Yes!" with my whole heart.

A canvas print of that day still hangs above our fireplace, featuring a canopy of trees and ferns surrounding us as the fall waters below sweep past us into a raging river. Jesse's guitar lies in its case with the lid wide open, as if beckoning us to sing. The photo shows us in a celebratory hug—my boots off the ground and my face hidden in Jesse's shoulder. It was the beginning of our life together and also the last time I would celebrate with no shadow of my mom's illness. We were separated and sheltered from the roar of the dangerous waters of cancer in that brief, beautiful moment. We did not know what was to come, but God did.

We get to say yes to the promises of God even when we do not know what the future holds. We can trust in what God says he will do, no matter what the circumstances we face, because Jesus sacrificed himself on our behalf. Jesus is the fulfillment of all of God's good and perfect promises to us, and he gives us hope that one day all of our hurts will be healed. He is the stone bridge that allows us to stand before the waterfalls of God's glory and be close to him. Do dangers still lurk on the other side of our holy moments of joy? Yes. Yet they cannot cross over and steal away the love of a promise accepted. Let me say that again: the darkness cannot cross over and steal away the love of a promise accepted.

All of God's promises are "yes" and "amen" because of who Jesus is and what he has done. He is the proposal and the proposed. He accepted God's promise to make things right, and he made us accepted by his sacrifice. His love was poured out like a waterfall falling across the rocks as he laid down his body for us. He hovered over the waters at the beginning of the world, and he walked across them when he was here on earth to prove he is the beloved of God.

Will you say yes? Or will you walk away? It is not going to be easy. In fact, it might be the most challenging path you've ever taken. But when you say "Yes!" to Jesus, you can trust in his coming "Amen." It's not simple or straightforward (it will be full of highs and lows you never saw coming), but in the end, all will be made right by Christ himself.

Dear God, all your promises are "yes" and "amen."

My deep need calls out to the deep kindness of your love (Psalm 42:7 TPT).

Your Holy Spirit reminds me of your faithfulness as I step out into the unknown.

I ask for the faith to believe that all your promises will be accomplished. Amen.

DAY 19

PRAYING ON OUR HARDEST DAYS

Daniel always prayed to God three times every day.
Three times every day, he bowed down
on his knees to pray and praise God.
—Daniel 6:10a ERV

It was my fourth day on a spring break mission trip when I decided to try kneeling during our morning devotional time. I was nineteen years old and hungry for a new experience of God. It was difficult to take that step toward being in the presence of God because there were so many voices telling me I shouldn't or that I would look silly. "OK, God, I'm going to try this," I said in my head.

I bent myself down, on two knees, between church pews so no one could see me. The carpet was an early '90s pattern of pastels that smelled like dust and stale coffee from generations of congregants before me. It had been a long time since I had knelt in prayer, and nobody was around to witness it. Growing up in Sunday school and church youth group, I often felt too embarrassed to kneel or too pressured to do so by a charismatic speaker. That day, there was no audience except God as slivers of morning light filtered through the stained-glass windows. In the silence, empty of outside expectations, I felt a peace and love surrounding me that felt like a warm hug after a long journey away from home. That moment was impactful, and I held on to it on my hardest days.

What started out as an uncomfortable spiritual practice of prayer became a lifeline in the days of early grief several years later. There were many days where I found myself curled up on my bed, numb with grief. Sometimes I would shift over to my knees for a moment and plead with God to take the pain away. Or I would ask for the strength to function through my day. Sometimes I would cry. My prayers were simple and short, but I knew God heard every single one of them.

We all have our own unique ways of talking to God, and it doesn't have to look the same for everyone. In the aftermath of grief, you may find that you don't have a lot of words to say to God, so maybe try changing your posture instead. Try praying standing up with your hands raised or kneeling on the ground if you're able. Or let your breath be a prayer of God, and as you breathe in and out deeply, remind yourself "God is love." Grief can make us draw our bodies inward into the fetal position, curled up into a ball, so try expanding your arms and limbs outward. Or while you're curled up on your bed, extend a single palm out like it's being held by someone right next to you.

The enemy may try to convince you that it doesn't matter, that you look silly, or that you're just "pretending" to be spiritual. But prayer in any form is powerful. God will lead you gently, and he'll encourage you to keep trying. I pray that he will surround you with a feeling of warmth and acceptance.

Dear God, here I am, with hands held high
or knees bent low.

I ask that you meet me here.

Even if I have little to say, every word is precious
to you.

Even if I don't always feel it, I know your presence is
surrounding me with love. Amen.

DAY 20

READY FOR GOOD GIFTS

Every good thing given and every perfect gift is from above, coming down from the Father of lights, with whom there is no variation or shifting shadow. —James 1:17 NASB

I sat in a black chair with my hands nervously clasped on top of the concrete table, my eyes staring daggers into the gold fleur-de-lis pattern inlaid into the corners. "There's no way I'm getting this job," I thought, looking over my paper résumé, which was lacking any food service experience.

"What have you been up to today?" the owner of the shop asked as perfunctory small talk to get the interview started.

"Well, I just deep cleaned my closet," I replied.

My mom had been gone for seven months, and I was once again unemployed. The nanny jobs I had found shelter in had respectfully ended, and I sat alone in our tiny, four-hundred-square-foot rental while my husband commuted to his full-time chemistry job. I was desperate to do something other than household chores or being left alone with my grief. One can only deep clean a closet so many times. I left the interview thinking, "Well, I'm glad I tried, but I'm probably not going to get it since I talked too much about my closet." I began catastrophizing in my head about how I could never show my face in the shop ever again or have another bite of their delicious cake.

When I got the call saying, "You got the job!" I laughed out loud. Guess why they hired me? Because I told them I deep cleaned my closet. Cleanliness is of high value and a requirement for a fast-paced dessert shop that could have a line going out the door many nights, and I would be surrounded by knives and frosting, flying in sweet clouds of chaos.

The transitions you go through after losing someone can take you places you never thought you would go. I didn't see myself working at a dessert shop, and I certainly didn't feel qualified. But God gave me such a pleasant surprise in this new job. Even amid the pain and confusion of loss, God still gives good gifts. The day I got the phone call telling me I got the job, I just had to laugh because the moments that felt utterly useless were the ones God was using to prepare me for the next good thing. My daily life was still very challenging and hard, but acknowledging this unexpected pocket of happiness reaffirmed God's unchanging character. My first day of training, I brought home a large slice of chocolate bliss cake—dark chocolate cake layers coated with cream cheese frosting. Jesse and I shared it together huddled over the kitchen counter. "Thank you, God, for this good gift," I said to myself.

Dear Father, you are the giver of good gifts.

Every good thing given and every perfect gift is from above.

Thank you for the moments where I am surprised and delighted by the opportunities you provide.

You write my ending, no matter how much I worry about the future.

Thank you for taking my chaos and bringing order to it. Amen.

DAY 21

FAITH TAKES HEART

Jesus turned, and seeing her he said, "Take heart, daughter; your faith has made you well." And instantly the woman was made well. —Matthew 9:22 ESV

The weekend after my mother's memorial service, I was standing inside a coffee shop perched on the edge of Bellingham Bay. The air was salty and tangy, with some sun peeking out on this July day. The waves were rolling in and out like they always do, and people happily milled about, ordering lattes and typing on their laptops. Suddenly, I felt someone reach out and touch my arm. My whole body became charged, and I visibly jumped, my brain screaming at me: "Who touched me?"

"Excuse me, can you tell me the time?" said a kind-looking, middle-aged lady. She looked at me expectantly, seeing my pale gold wristwatch gleaming in the sunlight.

"Oh, uh, 3:25 p.m.," I said in a daze. I had to breathe in and out slowly for a few minutes because my whole body was telling me that I was in danger. I was obviously not in any real danger, but for months after my mom died, my body could go into fight or flight mode—the physiological response our body has to perceived threats—and it was making me feel like I constantly needed to punch something or run away and hide. But the threat of grief, especially once the trauma of death has passed, is not a physical enemy we can take head on or run away from. So, what do we do?

Fight or flight responses can linger long after we've experienced trauma. For me, it took a couple of years before they faded, but everyone is different. Even now, when I see someone with a chemo head scarf, or when a friend loses a parent to cancer, I feel my body flood with anxiety.

In these moments where grief feels draining and overpowering, I look to the One who says, "Take heart, daughter" (Matthew 9:22 ESV). Jesus was talking to a woman who had been bleeding for twelve years, which made her ceremonially unclean and isolated from society. This woman reached out and touched the robe of the only one who could staunch the flow of pain and loneliness coursing through her veins. Jesus's whole being was filled with healing power, waiting for someone to reach out in faith. He was, is, and always will be sensitive to the touch of those who reach out to him for healing.

Reach out your hand and touch the hem of Jesus's cloak. Take heart. Even as you dwell in a body burdened by grief's idiosyncrasies that seem so sensitive to every shift and jolt, know that you follow a God who is even more attuned to your heart, grief, and body than you are.

Dear God, it can be so frustrating to navigate a grief
that doesn't respond the way I want it to.

I lay my fears and frustrations at the hem of your
cloak and offer them up to you.

Thank you for being a God who is attuned
to human suffering, who, through your Son,
lived as the Man of Sorrows, responding
with consistent compassion. Amen.

DAY 22

HOPE LIKE SEA GLASS

Make it your goal to live a quiet life, minding your own business and working with your hands, just as we instructed you before.
—1 Thessalonians 4:11 NLT

When my mother-in-law lost her mom after a long battle with Parkinson's disease, she began to collect sea glass. At every beach where she could find it, she gathered pieces of once sharp glass that had been eroded down to smooth triangles of iridescent light. They would change color when she shifted them in her hand. These pieces became precious to her, and she displayed them in glass vases and made jewelry from them.

If we let hope come back into our lives, it can start to wear away the sharp edges of our grief. You may have heard the old adage "time heals all wounds," but I haven't found it to be true for my own grief experience. Time alone is not enough to start healing, but some of the bitterness and pain I was carrying began to soften when I focused on simple tasks I enjoyed. These hobbies didn't "fix" anything overnight, but in time, they washed over my pain like small waves of the ocean and started to smooth the sting of my harshest feelings. Grief never completely goes away, but the acute sharpness of the pain ebbs and flows and doesn't stay the same forever. I think that God uses the simple joys of our life to insert hope into seemingly hopeless situations.

I rediscovered a love for watercolor painting when my mom got sick. The most freeing part is that watercolor is not easily controlled since the medium is, well, *water*. It flows all over the page and has a mind of its own. I could often hear my old art professor's instructions in my head as I painted: "Go with the flow of water." It was meditative to let go of control and let the paint flow where it wanted. It was also healing because, if you start crying while you're painting, you can just make it part of the artwork and let it fall on the paper! I felt like this simple hobby had spiritual lessons within it that I was subconsciously absorbing as I painted. As I learned to let go of having my painting go perfectly, it helped me remember I didn't need to grieve "perfectly" either.

We all have our own creative outlets, and now might be a good time to explore one that works for you. My mother-in-law collected sea glass. I dabbled in watercolor. Some people bake pies and cakes. Others take up a new sport or read books. Pick something that you genuinely like, that is low-stakes for you (not an area to judge yourself or accomplish anything), simply a place to get out of your head for a minute or two. If you try one thing and it makes you feel worse, just stop and try something else.

Paul, in 1 Thessalonians 4:13, says that we don't have to "grieve like people who have no hope" (NLT). He explains that if we believe that Jesus died and rose again, and that he will resurrect his children one day, then our grief has an end date. We remain here, alive and in grief. But one day, we will be reunited with God and never be separated from him again. This world breaks us apart into sharp shards of grief, but by choosing to continue living life and creating new things, we are letting hope get the final say. It doesn't matter how fancy or impressive your hobbies are but rather that you invite God's hope into them.

Dear Jesus, help me to live a quiet life of peace.

I know that, in you, I do not grieve without hope.

Guide me today to find healthy ways to fill my time.

Help me to see my time on this earth as a gift
and not a burden. Amen.

DAY 23

LOVE SPEAKS OUR NATIVE TONGUE

From now on, think of it this way: Sin speaks a dead language that means nothing to you; God speaks your mother tongue, and you hang on every word. You are dead to sin and alive to God. That's what Jesus did. —Romans 6:11 MSG

Señora Shelman, get better soon, OK? I don't like anybody else here," were the words written in messy handwriting in the bottom corner of a "get well soon" card. My mom rolled her eyes and laughed as she read it, telling me about the student who was a "handful" for everyone else but who would hang around her desk in her Spanish classroom to trade jibes and jokes. Somehow, my mom could be singing nursery rhymes in Spanish with handmade puppets one minute, and the next, she was enthralling her students with the story of the time she hid in a Bolivian supermarket during a riot, and thought she got shot, but had merely crushed the tomatoes in her bag. I learned my vowels, colors, and grammatical rules in Spanish before English as her daughter. I liked to joke that I was fluent in elementary school Spanish because my mom would rent Disney movies in Spanish for us, and my siblings and I would tag along for the neighborhood Spanish classes she would sometimes teach.

This is why my first Spanish class taught by someone else was such a shock. When it came time for the oral exam during my senior year of high school, I felt like a dog paddling upstream just to keep up with what my Spanish teacher was saying. Turns out, I wasn't particularly fluent in Spanish; I was just fluent in understanding my mom. Her gestures, quirks, and intonations were my native tongue. In her absence, I found I was missing the language I used to know so well. The jokes and stories. The knowing looks. In the absence of our loved one's presence, we can find ourselves drifting downstream without the familiar language we grew comfortable hearing.

I wonder sometimes about that student who connected with my mom. Did he ever find another safe corner in the high school after that? Did another teacher take him under their wing? Or did he wander in and out of classrooms, another number lost in the system? No matter what, I hope and pray that he remembered the love my mom showed him. In the same way my mom used language to connect with her students and children, God speaks to us. He knows our quirks and jokes, the places where we feel like we don't fit in. He traces back the roots of our words and understands the layers of meaning. One minute he scoops us up and tells us stories of Moses parting the waters, then David killing a giant, and Mary being brave as a teenager. The next moment, he enthralls us with the songs of the Psalms, where Asaph writes, "When my heart was grieved and my spirit embittered, I was senseless and ignorant; I was a brute beast before you. Yet I am always with you; you hold me by my right hand" (Psalm 73:21–23 NIV). He speaks to each one of us in our native tongue in love.

Dear Jesus, thank you for speaking words of life
over me.

You say that you are always with me
and that you hold me.

Help me to believe this today.

I'm listening to your words of encouragement,
and I hang on to every one. Amen.

DAY 24

GOD IS ALWAYS BESIDE ME

Teach these new disciples to obey all the commands I have given you. And be sure of this: I am with you always, even to the end of the age. —Matthew 28:20 NLT

We used to ride the horses in the field bareback," my mom told me during the commercial break of a daytime talk show we were watching. I had my textbooks balanced on my lap and was pretending to do homework, but really, I was listening to her tell stories. I imagined my mother and her four sisters trotting across the forested land owned by the lumber company next to their house. I could see in my mind their braids streaming behind them in the wind. Mom told me a haunting tale of grandpa's hunting dog getting loose and attacking their kitten. She also told me the story of their cow getting loose and eating all the prunes in the laundry room, leaving behind a cow-pie trail in the house.

Her stories of rural farm life were a world away from my suburban childhood with its mowed lawns and goldfish pets. Part of me felt torn as an eighteen-year-old, on the cusp of college, spending so much time at home listening to my mom's stories. I didn't know then that she would get sick with cancer and that I only had five years left to hear her stories. "Shouldn't I be out with my friends? Why are they not calling me back?" I would wonder. Like a glass dropped on the ground, shattering toward different corners of the room, my social circle was fracturing. I spent many afternoons watching daytime talk shows with my mom, sipping decaf tea on the faded futon couch. Stories of her past traumas, dating advice, and funny anecdotes poured out of her like salt from a Morton container, and I was seasoned by it. Looking back, it was the greatest gift. That time spent with my mom is so precious to me now.

When she died, I felt like that lonely teenager all over again. I was also going through other big life transitions at the time, such as being a recent college graduate and getting married. Grief felt like a runaway horse, charging through the beautiful scenery of these exciting life changes. Friendships I thought could weather anything became silent and ghostly. Other friends I hadn't talked to in years showed up at my doorstep like no time had passed. I also met others who had lost their mothers, whom I would have never connected with otherwise. As my relationship dynamics shifted and changed, there were times when I was hit with an overpowering sense of loneliness. I no longer had the familiarity and comfort of sitting beside my mom on a couch. Who could I turn to now?

Jesus spoke to me through the words of my sister in that season. One day, we were on a walk and she said to me, "Trina, it's time to go to counseling." I realized she was right. I needed more than my friendships could offer in this season. I needed a safe spot to sit and talk. It allowed me the freedom to not feel like a burden or a problem to be solved while pouring out my grief. Whether we are lonely or overwhelmed, Jesus can use the people around us to speak truth into our lives, whether that's a friend, a family member, or a counselor we trust. We're not meant to go through life alone, especially when we're grieving.

As I sank into the worn cushions of my counselor's couch a few weeks later, everything in me wanted to get up and run away. God spoke to me at that moment, and I felt like he said, "I'm with you always." In the same way I found comfort in sitting on the couch with my mom, Jesus sat with me that day as I did the brave thing and started to share my story. I was never alone.

Dear Jesus, You are always with me, no matter what.

Whether I'm surrounded by friends or alone
with no one to talk to, you are there.

Bring a friendly face into my path today to remind me
of your love and friendship toward me.

If I need a counselor, show me who to see
and what to do.

Help me to listen to wisdom. Amen.

DAY 25

BUOYED BY GOD'S LOVE

Your love, Lord, reaches to the heavens,
your faithfulness to the skies. —Psalm 36:5 NIV

I grew up catching palm-sized jellyfish with plastic grocery bags from the edges of our neighbor's barnacle-covered raft. Our hunting grounds were in a Puget Sound inlet just a short downhill walk from our house. We would have to push the raft across the sand to get it into the water each time we went jellyfish hunting. My siblings and I had so many adventures on that hunk of junk that I truly believed it was the Pacific Northwest's version of Huckleberry Finn's raft. One day, as we bent over the edge, looking into the water, trying to scope out jellyfish, I saw something with claws *move* out of the corner of my eye.

My siblings and I all started panicking, dancing around the three-by-five-foot raft as a large brown crab shuffled out from the coiled rusty rope in the corner where he had been hiding. We were hooting and hollering: "A crab! A crab! We're trapped!" The crab, nonplussed, moseyed its way around the deck until we got brave enough to scoop it into the water.

The crab was there the whole time, we just weren't aware of its presence. Grief can be the same way. It's lurking in the dark, waiting. Finally, it makes its presence fully known, sharp claws and all, in the wake of profound loss. When grief first appears, I need a moment to find my bearings. Once the initial shock fades, I'm full of fear. I'm afraid of it because it sneaks up on me, and it feels like I'm marooned in deep waters with no escape. I run around in a panic until I can slow down and process my grief.

After my mom died, I watched a lot of reruns of our favorite medical drama. I would come home from work, eat dinner with my husband, and then curl up in the corner of the couch. My mom and I had already watched them all, so I already knew who was going to die, fall in love, and which surgeries required a crash cart and ended with miraculous outcomes. It was repetitive and calming. One day, I realized I didn't want to watch the show anymore. I was ready to look grief straight in its beady little eyes and tell it to please stop pinching me so often. I was done with reruns and was ready again for uncharted waters. It was time to face the unresolved parts of my grief so I could continue on my way. I had danced around it for a time because that's what I needed in order to heal the tender parts of me, but it was time to become an explorer of life again.

God's love surrounded me as a child collecting jellyfish. His love was below me like the dark ocean waves lapping against the raft. His love stretched above me like the gray clouds in the sky. And God's love enveloped me when I was curled up on the couch, zoning out in front of a screen with my mother's memories held close. God's love has buoyed me up during every stage of my life and will continue to be there no matter what. When it was time to get off the couch, he reminded me that adventure was still out there, when I was ready.

Dear God, even if I make my bed in the darkest depths of the ocean, you are there.

If I rise on wings like a eagle, you are there.

To open myself up again to new opportunities and people seems foreign and scary, yet I know that your love for me is more powerful than any fear or hesitation I have.

You fill me up with your everlasting love and invite me to pour it back out to others. Amen.

DAY 26

FAITH BRINGS YOU BANANA BREAD

Be shepherds of God's flock that is under your care, watching over them—not because you must, but because you are willing, as God wants you to be; not pursuing dishonest gain, but eager to serve.
—1 Peter 5:2 NIV

Glenna and Steve were larger-than-life Sunday school teachers for the third graders at my church. Every Wednesday night, we were ushered in to pick out our name tags, and Glenna would smile at us with the tenderness of a grandma and the enthusiasm of a kindergarten teacher. Afterward, Steve would keep the entire crew enraptured with his epic tales of snake wrangling, racoon hunting, and outdoor adventures. He would often jump up and act out the various animals in his stories, reenacting epic chases and shenanigans. We were a bit disappointed when our parents picked us up because we wanted to hear the end of his stories. Together, they were the best of what Sunday school teachers should be—kind, warm, funny, and always safe.

Ffteen years later, I was surprised to find out that before Steve, Glenna had a husband who had passed away. I had found a handwritten note tucked in a plastic baggie of banana bread given to my dad about six months after my mom died. It was from Glenna, saying that she had lost her first husband and that she found that, around this time, people tend to forget about you; the meals, cards, and visits just stop. Everyone else has moved on, but you are, in many ways, just beginning to grieve. She sent banana bread to let my dad know that she had not forgotten him, and I have a feeling that she probably made this a practice for other widows and widowers. She knew what it was like to be alone.

Sometimes we get the banana bread, and sometimes it's our turn to give the banana bread. Sometimes we are the one suffering, and sometimes we are the one offering comfort. Jesus came to earth to serve us. He provided bread for those who were hungry and washed the feet of the disciples. He valued and remembered those who went unseen, which was completely different than the religious leaders at the time. Today, receive this thought: you are not alone three months after, three years after, or even three decades after sorrow.

Dear Lord, you know just what I need.

You comfort me and see my needs before I am aware of them.

You also empower me to comfort others.

When you walked among us on earth, you came as one who serves (Luke 22:27).

Help me to see and value others like you do. Amen.

DAY 27

HOPE KEEPS YOU HUMBLE

Likewise, you who are younger, be subject to the elders.
Clothe yourselves, all of you, with humility toward one another,
for "God opposes the proud but gives grace to the humble."
—1 Peter 5:5 ESV

In my small group at church, we talked about both the mundane and complex things of life. What does God have to say about anxiety? How do you know you are saved? Why do good people suffer? None of these discussions had easy answers. My husband and I were a part of an intergenerational small group, and I wouldn't have had it any other way. One of the members of our small group, named Mark, was in his eighties but he carried himself with the youthful energy of someone decades younger. Mark started many of his sentences with the same line:

"I might be wrong ..."

And then he would share some wisdom, an opinion he had, or some thoughts. He wore crisp, button-up shirts, his white hair was always well-groomed, and he offered to help me and my husband find an apartment when we were looking for housing. If we sat behind him at church, he would always turn around and give us a friendly wave. He never said anything disparaging about "this generation" or listed off his own troubles. For someone who said, "I might be wrong ..." so much, he seemed to get an awful lot right.

He was usually spot on when he spoke up, and he seemed to cut to the heart of any issue. Yet, those four little words ("I might be wrong") opened up the whole conversation. He was willing to be challenged, to see a new perspective, and to admit that he didn't have it all figured out. Initially, I had been dragging my feet about attending a small group. It was my first venture back into the church community after my mom had died, and my heart beat fast and I felt nauseous on the drive there. Could I trust this group? Could I let them in? All of my fears melted away as I entered our host's home and was greeted with the smell of warm gumbo on the stove and smiling faces gathered around the kitchen island. Our first discussion that night began with Mark's humble phrase, and I began to adopt it as my own.

My husband and I started quoting him all the time, smiling when we thought about his refreshing approach to discussions. We would say, "I might be wrong ..." when we talked about our feelings, shared a political opinion, or jokingly as we perused the grocery aisles for dinner choices. It was so good to remember that I might be wrong and that there was nothing *wrong* with admitting that. In fact, it was quite freeing. As a griever, I watched Mark approach life with curiosity and openness by asking questions instead of making judgments. I began to wonder, "How would my life change if I approached my own grief with curiosity?" I didn't have to get my grief "right" all the time or have all the answers. I could admit to other people I didn't have any of it figured out most of the time and open up the conversation to other points of view. I decided I wanted to live out the remaining decades of my life with a humility that drew people toward me instead of isolating myself from others, even though I was sometimes scared. As my dad liked to frequently say, I needed to "create dialogues instead of getting stuck in monologues."

Admitting I did not have it all together created space for me to see God's righteousness pour in. Where can you create space in your own life today to see God? Where can you say to him: "I might be wrong, but you are always right"? We hope in God and place our burdens and vulnerabilities in his hands. It is no longer our responsibility to have all the answers. People come to us just to talk because they know we will listen. My knowledge of grief and life is incomplete. I know that I will probably get quite a few things wrong along the way. But I also know that God is always right. He is always good. And I'm not wrong about that.

God, help me stay humble today and be open to starting conversations instead of dominating them.

Help me to remember that you oppose the proud but give grace to the humble.

Let me listen to your wisdom and surround me with people who seek you with humility. Amen.

DAY 28

LOVE IS FOUND IN TELLING OUR STORIES

Tell your children about it in the years to come,
and let your children tell their children. Pass the story down
from generation to generation. —Joel 1:3 NLT

I learned great storytelling by sitting at my grandparents' dining table. Filling up my plate with waffles, sausage, and homemade blackberry jam, I would sit back and listen as my papa began to narrate true stories from his life, which seemed to gather like smoke rings above my head. My papa, leaning back in his chair, would remove his brimmed cowboy hat, worn soft by days working in the barn, and say in his pepper and molasses voice,

"You know, in those days ..."

I would lean closer as he narrated his years spent as a cowboy, a carpenter, and a father of five girls and one boy. One time, he was bucked off a wild stallion, leaving a gnarly gash on his collarbone. He refused any numbing medication and took all sixteen stitches without saying a word. Another time, he collected several broken stop signs in the back of his truck because my mom knocked over so many while learning how to drive. He called up his buddy who worked for the city and had a good laugh before dropping them off to be repaired. He tamed a wild stallion no one else would dare approach. He struggled with addiction to alcohol and went to rehab in his seventies. He accepted Christ at eighty years old, after my grandma had prayed for him for decades. He never ran out of stories to tell because his life experiences were so vast.

My mother, like most people in her family, was also gifted in telling stories. She used to tell me about sneaking out the window with her sisters to stargaze on the roof in their pajamas, learning how to drive tour buses in Alaska by balancing a glass of water on the dashboard, and how she was temporarily engaged to a Mexican doctor while studying abroad, before meeting my dad. My mom and papa were some of the best storytellers out of all of us, and now that they're gone, my family remembers them by retelling their stories. My brother-in-law even has an affectionate nickname for it. He likes to say, "They're Shelman-niscing again," when us Shelmans start to reminisce about past stories. We trade memories like some people trade gifts or hugs, as small offerings of affection and a way to remember our shared heritage.

As Christians, we have our own shared history to remember. Sometimes I like to imagine people from the Bible, like Abraham or David, sitting next to me and sharing their stories. Abraham could tell me about the time God told him he would be a father at the age of ninety-nine. Or maybe he would tell me about how he almost stabbed his son in the heart at the top of the mountain until God stopped him at the last minute and offered up a ram instead. Maybe David would tell me about grabbing a lion by its mane and striking it down, or taking down a giant with only a stone and a slingshot. Maybe they would tell me some of their regrets too. Lies, betrayal, murder, and the children whom they failed. They were real people, with real joys and losses. These are the people God included in his family tree, eventually leading to the birth of Jesus.

People like David, Abraham, Ruth, and Esther are all part of our spiritual family. We can reminisce about God's character and faithfulness together. Our lives may look a lot different than theirs did, but we are still being asked to face our own giants, lay down dreams and desires we have, and wrestle with grief too. When Jesus came and sacrificed himself, he made a way for us to become a part of his family. Now we know how the story of the Bible ends—that it will not end in death but with Jesus returning in victory. The books of the Bible are not just stories, but real inspiration and guidance for our own lives.

As I struggle with my grief, I like to remember the closeness and warmth of my grandparents' breakfast table—a place where stories were exchanged, debated, and expected. I don't know what heaven is going to look like, but sometimes I like to imagine there will be a big table with lots of waffles. I like to imagine Jesus sitting beside me, leaning back in his chair, and saying, "You know, in the beginning was the Word ..." and then proceeding to tell me the whole redemptive story.

Dear God, I can't wait to sit beside you and hear what you have to say.

When I feel alone in my story, help me to remember that I have a great adoptive family to share my story with.

Help me to be brave and continue telling others about you even as I grieve. Amen.

DAY 29

IMPERFECT GRIEVING

Dear brothers and sisters, when troubles of any kind come your way, consider it an opportunity for great joy. For you know that when your faith is tested, your endurance has a chance to grow. —James 1:2–3 NLT

My mom and I made Spritz cookies, chocolate-dipped pretzel sticks, and reindeer cookies together in the kitchen during the holidays. The Spritz cookies were usually a tad burnt, the pretzel sticks were not uniform in their application of chocolate, and the reindeer antlers were always crooked. We were not aiming for perfection; we were more chaotic and freewheeling. After my mom died, when it came time for my dad to move out of his house, my sister and I volunteered to pack up the kitchen. We opened up a kitchen drawer full of wrappers, food dye, and festive cookie cutters. Each object represented a future project my mom wanted to try. Just looking at these deferred dreams took my breath away for a minute. My mom took great joy in cooking projects, and her kitchen was infused with her passion.

Perfectionism was never the goal. It was about joy.

As we continued packing, I found my mom's old cookbooks. Tucked inside one was a scrap of paper with a short recipe for pancakes. Below the recipe, written in her loopy cursive, she had listed ways to watch Don Quixote with her her Spanish students. A list of student assignments was printed on the other side. This paper breathed the life she lived. Her notes were written in ink, but they were also written on my heart as I remembered all the dreams she had. I remembered when we had seen a production of *Man of La Mancha* (a musical version of Don Quixote), and we had sung "The Impossible Dream" the whole car ride home. My mom had so many wonderful dreams. Who would carry them forward now?

There is no right way to grieve, but I had to try to grieve in the best way I knew how. After helping my dad, I took home my mom's old recipe books. From time to time, I would pull them down from the shelf if I needed inspiration for dinner or a good cry. I would pull out the scraps of paper she wrote recipes and class ideas on and leaf through them like they were pages in her diary. Even though my mom was no longer alive, I could take her memories along with me. I could remember her in the recipes I would try, the dreams I would continue to dream, and in embracing the imperfections of my grieving process. But this didn't happen overnight. In fact, it took years for me to get there.

How can you move on without the other person? How can you live your own life without abandoning your loved one's dreams? God knows our hurts and pains. He asks us to trust that his plan for us will produce perseverance and that we can have joy in his promise of restoring us. He reminds us in his word that faith, hope, and love remain. Love is always patient and kind and is not in a hurry. We don't need to rush to figure out our grief. We don't need to feel guilty for continuing on. For no matter what, we know that God is with us, and he helps us find the joy in our lives again.

As I made my mom's old recipes, I cried tears of sorrow, and tears of remembrance. I made Spritz cookies, chocolate-dipped pretzel sticks, and crooked reindeer cookies. It wasn't the same without her, but slowly and surely, I learned to embrace the joy of imperfection.

Dear God, help me to stop trying to pursue the perfect idea of what grieving should look like and, instead, focus on what I already know to be true.

Impossible dreams start to become possible when I rely on you.

Give me a vision for your plans for me.

Be with me today. Amen.

DAY 30

SUSTAINED BY DAILY BREAD

Jesus said to them, "I am the bread of life. Whoever comes to me will never be hungry, and whoever believes in me will never be thirsty." —John 6:35 NRSV

One of my childhood obsessions was bread. I thought a lot about Costco bulk rolls. When my grandma made me homemade bread, I could not get enough. People often commented to my mom, "This kid loves bread!" I used to sit on the counter to watch bread rise in the view-window of my mom's bread machine, anticipating the minute it would finally be ready. I still can't resist a fresh slice from the oven. In the Bible, bread is used as a metaphor for life. Bread sustains us, and it is essential for our bodies. This is true for every culture in every part of the world. We need some form of carbohydrate to live, and we need it daily.

On a previous day, we talked about how God chose to tell his story through Abraham's family, who were called the Israelites. Long after Abraham died, his family grew into a large people group that had miraculously been freed from slavery in Egypt. God had sent plagues and wonders to get the stubborn pharaoh of Egypt to let them go. Now, as they wandered in the desert and their stomachs began to rumble, they started to forget that God had already proven himself to them over and over again. They were finally free, but they hungered for more and were not satisfied. Could God be trusted to sustain them? Would he provide sustenance in the dry and barren desert? They complained and doubted that God would be there for them.

After my mom died, I asked myself some of the same questions the Israelites had asked. I felt like grief had set me down in a dry spiritual desert, and God seemed far away, unconcerned with my troubles. Even though he had shown up in my life in miraculous ways in the past, it was so hard to see beyond my daily needs as a grieving person. One of the wedding gifts I received was a small metal tray with a loaf of bread etched into it that said, "Give us this day our daily bread," and I had placed it above our stove. One day, I looked at it and realized that God would provide enough for me for that day. Even though it felt like I was in the desert, God had not forgotten me.

God did not forget about the Israelites either. He provided miraculous bread called manna that rained down from heaven that they could collect and eat each day. If they hoarded this bread, it would be spoiled by the next day, so they had to rely on God every single day to provide what they needed. The Israelites were still learning how to trust God to provide, just as I am still learning how to trust God to provide for me in my grief. I am tempted to hoard resources, in case he doesn't show up this time.

Deep down, I am still on the hunt for my own bread—for things that will give me comfort and sustenance. I still hold my breath and wait for God to show up.

Perhaps you can relate. You, too, are looking for some sustenance to get you through. Will there be enough? Will he see you through? Who will you be a few months down the road? These are some of the questions you might be asking yourself. Like the Israelites, we don't know how long our own spiritual deserts will last. But we do know the God who brings daily bread, who asks, "Will you trust me? Will you accept my provision?" God rained down bread from the sky every morning for his people. I imagine that this bread covered the ground like a flaky dew—miraculous, yet practical. Like manna from heaven, God is miraculous and also incredibly personal when he provides for our practical needs.

Dear God, be my daily bread, providing sustenance
and energy for my weary soul.

You are the Bread of Life, and when I come to you,
I never go away hungry or thirsty.

You see both my practical and spiritual needs
and provide for them.

I love you. Amen.

PART 2

FAITH, HOPE, LOVE

God uses faith, hope, and love to build resiliency into our grief as we open ourselves up to new and good things.

DAY 31

FAITH WALKS ON WATER

When the disciples saw him walking on the water, they were terrified. In their fear, they cried out, "It's a ghost!" But Jesus spoke to them at once. "Don't be afraid," he said. "Take courage. I am here!" —Matthew 14:26–27 NLT

What is the significance of Jesus walking on the water? I've always been fascinated by the illustrations in children's Bibles of Jesus calmly strolling on top of the water as his disciples gawk at him from inside their boat. I wondered about this story for many years: "Why did Jesus walk on water?" It started to make sense to me when one of the pastors at our church explained that the sea and water represented chaos to people back then. When Jesus walked across the water as if it were solid ground, he was showing them that he was, indeed, God—the God who brings calm and centers the turbulence of our anxious hearts.

Peter, one of Jesus's disciples, couldn't help but challenge Jesus and respond, "If it's really you, and not a ghost, ask me to come join you." Jesus responds, "Come," and does something completely different than any other god of that time: he reaches out his hand to Peter. Jesus is the God who strolls upon chaos and, by taking Peter's hand, enables Peter to walk beside him without sinking under the waves. When Peter looks down at the wind and waves, he is terrified. He sees the forces of chaos, destruction, and death, and starts to sink. But when he looks back to Jesus, he is saved.

Sometimes, around 4 a.m., I lie awake and think about my questions for God. "If you're really good, why do bad things happen?" "If you're really God, why did my mom die?" Like Peter, I step up to the edge of the boat and throw my questions overboard as a challenge to God to see what he will say in return. Oftentimes, instead of answering my questions directly, God reminds me of the personhood of Jesus. He says to me, "Come. Come out into the water and walk with me." Even if I sink a little bit underneath my own hesitations and fears, he never abandons or leaves me.

In *The Message*, Eugene Peterson paints this scene beautifully between Jesus and Peter, writing, "Jesus didn't hesitate. He reached down and grabbed his hand. Then he said, 'Faint-heart, what got into you?' " I love that Peterson writes it as "Jesus didn't hesitate," because it reminds me that Jesus does not delay comforting me. Even when I am reluctant or afraid, Jesus brings peace. I like to imagine him walking toward me, above the chaos, in the early hours of the morning.

Dear God, you are bigger than the chaos happening in my life right now.

You tell me, "Take courage! I am here." Jesus, you bring peace to my mind as I lie awake with questions.

You do not hesitate or delay to comfort me.

I love you. Amen.

DAY 32

HOPE LIKE A LION, HOPE LIKE A LAMB

The Lord will roar like a lion from Jerusalem; his loud voice will thunder from that city, and the sky and the earth will shake. But the Lord will be a safe place for his people, a strong place of safety for the people of Israel. —Joel 3:16 NCV

My third summer working at a summer camp, I transitioned from counselor to a behavioral support position. This summer camp was unique because many of the kids had emotional or behavioral challenges, and my new position meant I would step in when the counselors needed extra support or leadership. One of the first graders bonded with me and always wanted to sit next to me at lunch. He would run across the cafeteria every day to give me a hug, yelling, "Katrina! Katrina!" He confessed to me one day that he felt like the Hulk character because he would feel calm and sweet one moment and then like a raging monster the next. He didn't feel like he could control his emotions. I couldn't help but be endeared to this little boy who would follow me like a shadow one minute and then cuss me out with a lisp later that day.

One challenging day, we were at a beautiful park right next to Bellingham Bay. As we were packing up to go, he bolted up the trail next to the cliffside. I started to chase him as I was frantically using my walkie-talkie to get ahold of another counselor for backup and praying to God he would stay safe. Suddenly on the path before me was a large garter snake. I stumbled back in surprise and fear. I've always been scared of snakes. But there was no time for my phobia, and I jumped across the snake while calling out the child's name. Finally, I caught up to him and, by talking to him about his siblings and how much he loved them, I convinced him to let me carry him back to the van. He fell asleep on my shoulder on the ride back to camp. My hands couldn't stop shaking because adrenaline was still pumping through my body. "I'm not cut out for this," I thought to myself. But looking back, I see someone who did the best they could in a stressful situation.

When my mom died, it felt like death was a large and ugly snake in my path. I couldn't ignore it or run away from it; I had to face it. I had to keep going with my life and accept that my mom was really gone. When I think back to that challenging day at the park, I see God with me, roaring like a lion to back me up. I faced three of my biggest fears that day: heights, snakes, and something bad happening to someone I cared about. If God was with me that day, he could be with me during my worst days of grief. God is a fierce protector, and he will chase you down no matter what dangers surround you. He is powerful and worthy of awe. On the days when fear lies in your path, God gives you the courage to jump over it and continue on.

Dear God, thank you for being there with me during my most challenging moments.

I don't have to face my fears by myself, and that's a huge comfort to me.

You are the lion that triumphs over death and wipes away all of my tears. Amen.

DAY 33

LOVE SAYS GOODBYE

If God hadn't been there for me, I never would have made it.
—Psalm 94:17 MSG

I was the first one to notice that my mom was dying. We all knew there was nothing left to do for her, medically speaking, because the cancer had spread too far. We had begun slowly saying goodbyes over that last week. The hospice nurse had left me an "end-of-life symptoms" pamphlet, and I clung to the information like a shipwrecked sailor. I was sinking beneath the waves, and there was little to buoy me up. But if I hadn't read that pamphlet, I would've missed her last breath, and my family wouldn't have had the opportunity to say one last goodbye.

When I was in college, I went on a mission's trip to the UC Davis college campus in California during my spring break. During that trip, we spent time walking around campus, starting up conversations with strangers about faith. My friend Jasmine and I were walking the beautiful arboretum on campus, which is full of bridges that look like Claude Monet paintings with canals and sweeping branches over winding paths full of blooming flowers. We ran into an elderly gentleman walking his little, white dog. We asked if we could discuss what faith is to him and what he put his faith in, and he politely obliged. He told us, "I'm a Christian. I have faith in God. I don't doubt him for a second. I lost my wife a couple years ago, and God showed me purple sparkles raining down from heaven on her deathbed. And it brought me so much comfort because that was always her favorite color." He smiled as he remembered this story, and he said it with such intensity that you couldn't look away. I'm still not sure why he was so open with his story that morning, but it stuck with me for a while. Did he really see purple sparkles? Did God do that? But it left me with the more important questions such as: Where is God when people die? Is he there? Are his angels waiting in the wings?

People asked me frequently after my mom died, "Was her passing peaceful?" and I would always nod and say, "Oh yes, very peaceful," because I didn't know what else to say. But really, it was more complicated than that because the fragments of our grief rained from the heavens and stuck to every inch of my family's skin, and we could never shake it it off. It was not peaceful in the way God calms the sea, but in the way he tore the curtain of the temple after he died and the sky broke out in thunder after Jesus yelled out, "My God, my God, why have you forsaken me?" It was the passing of a life well-lived and accepted into heaven, and the tears of a family left behind. Breaking, thundering, raining, and then silence.

Whether the last moments of your loved one's life consist of supernatural comfort or unspeakable chaos, an important question you may find yourself asking God is: Where were you? Were you in that space?

As I held my mom's hand and said goodbye, I remembered the purple sparkles of a grieving widower walking his dog in the beautiful shelter of the arboretum on a warm spring day. I did not see signs or visions that day, I only heard a voice telling me: It's time to say goodbye. If God had not been there in that moment, I never would have made it.

Dear God, I don't have many words today.

Processing these moments is painful.

Sit with me in this hard memory today. Amen.

DAY 34

THE PROVISION OF CHRIST

When they had all had enough to eat, he said to his disciples, "Gather the pieces that are left over. Let nothing be wasted."
—John 6:12 NIV

"Can I have another cookie please? I dropped mine," I said, looking up at the card table where two elderly church ladies smiled down at me during summer Vacation Bible School. They quickly placed another large chocolate chip cookie into my small palm. I was four years old and was elated to get another free cookie. "I could do this forever!" I thought to myself as I schemed. I would eat most of a cookie, drop it, and then ask for another one. My plan was to recruit other kids in the preschool group until we all had two cookies. Thankfully, before I could enact the next steps of my plan, it was time to move on to arts and crafts. I was saved from starting my own preschool crime ring that day, and I forgot about this memory for many years. I was reminded of it, however, when I was tempted to start bargaining with God as a griever. "Could I convince him to bring my mom back if I sacrificed something big?" I would often think to myself.

"Can I get another mom, please? I lost mine," I would plead in the darkness. Perhaps if I tried hard enough or proved to God that I had learned whatever "lesson" grief was supposed to teach me, this nightmare would end. Sometimes I treated God like a kind church lady who I had to occasionally manipulate to get what I wanted. Other times, I viewed him as a strict Sunday school teacher who would yell at me for climbing trees or just *looking* like I was thinking about trouble. None of these imperfect images of God was helping with my grief.

As I tried to bargain with God, I remembered the story of him feeding the five thousand and how, after everyone had eaten their fill, there were still twelve baskets left over. He spoke to me through Jesus's words in this story: "Gather the pieces that are left over. Let nothing be wasted" (John 6:12 NIV). I didn't need to bargain with, convince, or cajole a God who fed thousands until they were completely satisfied from five loaves of bread with leftovers to spare. He was already there, providing for my needs.

The Jesus in this story stands in stark contrast to the false ideas we sometimes have about God. In the absence of our loved ones, he gives us what we need. We don't need to scheme or plot to be provided for. He is already aware of all our wants, needs, and desires. God is our giver, sustainer, and provider. He is a God who says, "Let nothing be wasted."

Dear God, can I have another portion
of your presence?

Mine feels depleted today.

You offer unwarranted generosity and second chances
in abundance.

You have "delivered my soul from death, my eyes from
tears, my feet from stumbling" (Psalm 116:8 BSB).

Thank you. Amen.

DAY 35

REMAIN RECEPTIVE TO GOD'S PEACE

Peace I leave with you, My peace I give to you; not as the world gives do I give to you. Let not your heart be troubled, neither let it be afraid. —John 14:27 NKJV

Growing up as a middle child, I purposefully lost the "shotgun" battle with my siblings and rarely sat in the front seat. When they yelled out, "Shotgun!" and ran to claim the coveted front seat, I would linger behind, keeping my voice from adding to the chaos. I didn't mind the backseat most days. I liked sitting near the window, counting the telephone poles we passed or spying on unsuspecting drivers as they sang to music alone in their car or scratched their noses. Nobody seemed to notice my towhead peeking out of the window, observing the world from the backseat. I thought I was choosing peace. But really, I was holding onto the little bit of power I had so that when the random day came that I wanted to sit in the front seat, I could play my trump card, and my mom would say, "Trina wants to sit up front today, guys. She never sits up here," and no one could argue with her. I liked that feeling of control, knowing I could choose to sit in the front seat on the days when I wanted a different view.

God is the Lord of order and perfect peace. He is the only one who can put everything in its right order, in complete wholeness with everything else. In our daily lives, we get glimpses of his perfection. When I took art lessons as a child, during the last session of the summer, the art teacher would let us pile into her convertible car to get ice cream cones. I remember the wind whipped my hair into a frenzy as I ate my ice cream, and I thought, "I'm so cool right now." This happy memory is just a small taste of what God's peace will one day be like. I don't fully know what it will be like, but I'm excited and anxious to experience it.

Because I'm not the true source of peace, I can't force it into my own life. God is the source, originator, and sustainer of peace. When my mom died, I was only twenty-three, and death seemed to disrupt all of the plans I had for my life. When I told my counselor about my anger over losing my mom so young, she reminded me that we live in a broken world where things are not right. I don't have control over when people die, and it isn't my job to fix that. I don't have to be *at peace* about losing my mom, but I can, instead, seek out a God who freely gives peace. I can give up control and let God give me a different view.

Dear God, most days I feel anything but peaceful.

On those days you tell me: "Let not your heart be troubled, neither let it be afraid" (John 14:27 NKJV).

In this broken and fallen world, you are the source of a peace which transcends all understanding.

I'm anxious for the day when you make everything right. Amen.

DAY 36

FAITH REMEMBERS ITS ROOTS

A bruised reed he will not break, and a smoldering wick he will not snuff out, till he has brought justice through to victory. In his name the nations will put their hope. —Matthew 12:20–21 NIV

During one of my first visits home after my mom died, I pulled up the car to see my dad standing in his front garden, watering a tall lily plant. The once stark patch of soil was overflowing with succulents, lilies, and blushing roses. The front porch was framed with bright pink blooms and tall grasses swaying nearby. When my mom was sick, every inch of their kitchen counter was covered with plants gifted from family and friends. Why do people give you so many plants when someone is sick or dies? In all honesty, I killed a lot of the plants that people gave me. My dad was not like me.

He took each beautiful flower and bit of greenery covering his kitchen counter and placed them in the dark ground. He collected the dead leaves and watered the tiny shoots that reached toward the sun. He transplanted the good tidings of his friends into a small garden of love. He planted the grief flowers outside his house, and that small explosion of colors and textures became a memorial to the bright and fierce lady we all lost. It took my breath away when I first saw it. I recognized the lilies, roses, and daffodils that had sat on the countertop for so long and were now growing in the freedom of healthy soil.

She was gone, and yet, in those flowers, and my dad's care for them, she still bloomed. The roots of who she was and who she had been continued to bring beauty into the world. I didn't fully see it back then, because I wasn't ready to accept the regrowth, transplanting, and pruning that grief requires, but appreciating the beauty of my dad's efforts was a start.

It can be so tempting to treat grief like a problem that needs to be fixed rather than a plant that needs to be carefully transplanted into new soil. Like those flowers my dad lovingly put into his front yard, Jesus tends to our grief with the same gentle care. In Matthew 12:20, Jesus is described as someone who does not break a bruised reed, which reflects his character of gentleness and faithfulness. There are no easy solutions to our pain, and we will always miss our loved ones. There is no avoiding or diminishing that fact. But perhaps, with time and cultivation, we can begin to recognize the small signs of life returning.

Dear Jesus, thank you for tending to me with care and kindness.

You don't break the bruised reed, and neither will you be harsh with me in my grief.

Transplant this grieving ache I carry into your soil so that I can see my faith grow. Amen.

DAY 37

HOPE FIGHTS LIKE A MOTHER

The Lord *is your mighty defender, perfect and just in all his ways;*
Your God is faithful and true; he does what is right and fair.
—Deuteronomy 32:4 GNT

Rodney was tall, mean, and walked like he owned the whole block. He and his friends had a hideout in the woods at the end of our cul-de-sac where they would practice throwing knives and try to get away from us younger neighborhood kids. One day, my sister and her friend were hanging out near a tree, and Rodney started throwing rocks at them. They ran away, terrified, and told my mom the whole story. It has been said not to mess with a mama bear's cubs if you don't want to get mauled, and the same was true of my mother. Rochelle "Shelly" Shelman, did not back down from a fight when the vulnerable were under attack.She said, "I will take care of it," in a calm but determined tone I had never heard before in my life—not even when I toppled the wooden dollhouse and it smashed to smithereens. She marched down the middle of the road in her '90s-style jean shorts and a baggy sweatshirt with a fiery trail of mama anger following in her wake. Looking back, I kind of feel bad for Rodney because he was no match for her. My mom, even though she was six inches shorter than him, walked right up to him and said, "Don't you *ever* mess with my kids *again*!" She came back home, and we jumped up and down in celebration, retelling the story with great embellishment for days. She was our neighborhood hero, and we were in awe.

My grief has reminded me in some ways of that neighborhood bully. I have felt like grief was trying to push me around and tell me how to live my life, but this time, I didn't have my fiercest advocate to back me up. My mom was in heaven, and she couldn't march down and set things straight anymore. There were so many days where I asked God, "Can you be like my mom for me today?" It wasn't the same as my mom's physical presence, but it helped to know that God still had my back. Even though I am an adult, I still need someone to care and fight for me in the maternal way that good mothers do for their children.

Perhaps you've lost someone who was your biggest advocate and cheerleader. They can't be replaced, and you deeply feel their absence. I pray that God would be your defender today and that you would have confidence in his love and support for you.

Dear God, you tell me, "The LORD will fight for you; you need only to be still" (Exodus 14:14 NIV).

So here I am, still before you, asking you to be my defender today.

When my grief grows into discouragement and confusion, fight for me and remind me who I really am.

You are faithful and true. Amen.

DAY 38

LOVE SAYS, "I WILL GUIDE YOU"

The Lord *says, "I will guide you along the best pathway for your life. I will advise you and watch over you."*
—Psalm 32:8 NLT

In the days, weeks, and months that followed my mother's death, I felt like I was living in a haze of wildfire smoke. She died on June 20—the day before the first official day of summer. Wildfires were raging in Canada that year and spilled over into Washington state, which brought with them a heat wave. Everything around me felt cloudy, smoky, and suffocating.

My whole family loaded up into my dad's truck along with cheap inner tubes that reeked of plastic. We floated down the Deschutes River, and for a moment, I forgot my mom was dead. The cold water shocked my system, and I could hear my husband and brother-in-law yelling in protest. My sister and I both laughed at their reluctance to jump in. We had grown up diving headfirst into the Puget Sound, which never truly warmed up. After floating down this natural lazy river several times, I felt buoyed from the depths of grief.

This temporary lull was soon interrupted. On the way home, we stopped at Ralph's Thriftway for hamburger buns. We ran into someone from church who said hello and that they were sorry my mom died. I stood there gripping the plastic tie of the hamburger buns in my hand, still wearing my swimsuit underneath my damp T-shirt. I looked like someone going to a backyard BBQ, not someone who was grieving the recent death of their mom. "Are they judging me for doing fun summer activities?" I thought to myself. But as I got into the car, I realized that I was doing exactly what my body and brain needed. I couldn't tell you what was happening in the news, what day of the week it was, or even begin to think about my plans for the fall. I could only focus on the next concrete thing: what will I have for dinner? What movie should I watch? It was a summer of confusion, brain fog, and recovering from the exhaustion of caring for someone who was dying. I was fortunate to have that time to heal without pressuring myself to process what was coming next.

After Jesus rose from the dead, he appeared to his followers a handful of times and promised them that this was not the end but, rather, the beginning of something new. He would ascend to the Father, and the Holy Spirit would come as a Comforter. The disciples were grieving the loss of their leader, but something greater was coming in the form of the Holy Spirit. It was a plan they couldn't have imagined in their wildest dreams. That gift of God's constant presence and guidance is still available to us today. If you feel lost and adrift, look to the Spirit for comfort and know that God has a pathway for your life, even if it's not what you might expect.

I couldn't have faced the next season of my life without the Holy Spirit. As the skies began to clear, and the summer sun faded, I realized I needed to prepare for what was next. It was time to find a job and to start figuring out what my life looked like without my mom. God began putting people and opportunities in my life that were exactly what I needed. I still felt confused and burdened by grief, but there were also new adventures awaiting me. My friend asked me to volunteer to watch babies for the mom's group at church. My friends from high school visited me, and I showed them around my town. Most importantly, God reminded me to give myself grace to take as much time as I needed to figure out what the future looked like. He did not judge me or rush me during this time. He was there to guide me and show me new paths to take, no matter how lost or cloudy my future seemed.

Dear God, you guide me along the best path for my life.

I don't know what life will look like amid grief and feeling lost, but I'm willing to try to figure it out with you by my side.

I can't do this without you.

I trust that you will watch over me as I move forward. Amen.

DAY 39

GOD'S CHARACTER REMAINS CONSTANT

Jesus Christ is the same yesterday, today, and forever.
—Hebrews 13:8 NKJV

One day I stood beside the small strip of countertop we called a kitchen in our rental house and stared at measuring cups. I just kept staring at them. Then I started to cry, and I told my husband, "I can't bake. I can't do it." Baking without my mom didn't feel right. When I made my first batch of cookies, she drove to the corner store to get me milk because I thought the batter was too dry. I didn't know then that cookies spread in the oven, but she trusted my judgment and supported me anyways, even when they spread like pancakes on the cooking sheet. I have improved since then, successfully making cakes, cookies, bars, and muffins many times over. Baking used to be my escape. Baking was something I had shared with my mom, with aprons double-tied around our waists and ingredients scattered across the counters. "Who will I become if I can't bake? What is the point of trying without her?" I thought to myself as my tears ran down.

My friend Kamille had a similar experience after her brother died. She was a passionate and talented cook. She taught cooking classes, blogged recipes, and hosted multicourse dinner parties at her table. Yet, in her grief, she found herself being pulled away from the kitchen and into the garden. She soon became a dahlia enthusiast, attending local dahlia grower meetups. She couldn't get enough of vibrant blooms, tangled root balls, and plotting out garden spaces. She told me, "I might come back to cooking again someday, but for now the garden is where I belong." Her heart found healing and purpose in the soil in a way that her old interests couldn't serve her. She was different because of her grief, but at the same time, the passionate and talented person she was before remained.

I was alarmed and saddened by the fact that baking no longer brought me joy but rather pain. I thought I would never be able to pick up those measuring cups again. But seeing Kamille's open-handedness with her pursuits made me realize it was alright to set some things down for the time being. Maybe I would bake again someday, but during that time it wasn't what I needed. God put her in my life at just the right time to show me what remained in my life. I was deeply loved and seen by God, even as my interests changed. I was changing, but his character remained the same.

In this time of pruning, I realized that I had wrapped up parts of my identity into baking. Being a good baker like my mom was a core part of who I thought I was. When baking no longer appealed to me, I found myself asking, "Who am I?" God helped me realize that what I really loved about baking was creating something beautiful out of ingredients that were not inherently beautiful. Taking piles of dusty flour and cracked eggs and coming out with glossy chocolate brownies. God had created me to be passionate about cultivating beauty and meaning out of seemingly random things or ideas.

Just like Kamille, God invites us to discover which parts of ourselves remain in the wake of grief. God is the constant in our lives as we navigate our new identities in him.

Dear Jesus, you are the same yesterday, today, and forever.

I can rely upon you to guide me because your character is constant.

Help me to have openhandedness about activities which you might be calling me to set aside for now.

You created me to create meaning out of random and broken things in order to encourage myself and others.

Help me to remember that today. Amen.

DAY 40

DANCING TO A NEW RHYTHM

Work willingly at whatever you do, as though you were working for the Lord rather than for people.
—Colossians 3:23 NLT

The fall right after my mom died, my friend Kristi recommended that I work as a nanny. She told me, "You can show up in comfy pants, and you get to hold babies!" I took her advice and soon found myself chasing after little ones, sweeping up fish cracker crumbs, and making block towers. This was a pivot from my original plan. I had my teaching degree and had always envisioned I would go straight into teaching as a newlywed. I had dreams of spending long, fulfilling days teaching young minds and calling my mom afterward to decompress. Those dreams didn't look the same without my mom. Nannying was the right spot for me at that time. I chose resilience over striving.

Resilience is about being flexible and adaptable to tough situations in order to find a path forward to healing. It's not about bouncing back to exactly who or what you were before. Instead of beating myself up for not advancing my "career," I had to stop and realize that I was still using all of the skills I learned to get that degree: persistence, management of young minds, communication with parents, and planning developmentally appropriate activities.

One day, I was listening to an upbeat folk song as I bounced a baby on my hip in time with the music, and a new thought washed over me: grief had given me a totally different perspective. All of the things I had been worried about before my mom was sick didn't matter to me anymore. I used to worry about getting ahead in my career, coordinating a perfect home setup, and worrying what other people thought about me. When I got the phone call that my mom had tumors in her brain, all of the clutter of life was pushed aside. I had to become resilient in response to immense stress because there wasn't any other option. After she died and the stress of illness was gone, I still needed that resilience.

As I danced across the kitchen, the young child in my arms started to giggle. God spoke to me at that moment: "You are exactly where you need to be." I was exactly where I needed to be because I was dancing to the rhythms of God's grace, not clinging to old dreams. Yes, it was important to grieve those losses and acknowledge that this was not what I expected. When all of the bottles were washed, toys put away, and the baby was fast asleep during naptime, I began to dream a new dream of being a writer. In college, I had taken a creative nonfiction class and had briefly considered being a writer. That day, I picked up my phone and began to type out little essays about my grief. Those thoughts were the beginning of this book you now hold in your hands. If I had known that then, I would have been completely overwhelmed by the idea. Instead, God carefully led me from one writing opportunity to another like a tower of wooden blocks carefully constructed by the Creator himself.

In college, I felt like I was always busy pursuing the next, right opportunity. Almost every hour of my day was scheduled and packed with an assignment, internship, job, or mentorship. Now my days stretched endlessly in front of me, and I had no idea what I would do once this nanny job ended. But in that moment, dancing with a giggling baby, God showed me he is not concerned with productivity but, rather, connectivity. He invited me to choose to listen to wisdom instead of chasing the next big thing. I will always be grieving, and that's a tough reality to face. But God gave me the gift of his grace—grace to pursue, to adapt, to take joy in the small things, to dance to a new rhythm.

God knows exactly what we need and doesn't always reveal more than we need to know in the moment. God doesn't reveal the mystery of our future and that can be frustrating at times. But whatever he has for us in the moment is an opportunity to work as if for the Lord and not for those around us—to choose resilience over striving.

Dear Jesus, create in me a resilient heart bent toward you.

Help me to work willingly for you, whether that's as a nanny, a writer, a teacher, or whatever job you've called me to in that season.

Instead of chasing the next opportunity, help me to pursue you. Amen.

DAY 41

FAITH IS A FOUNTAIN OF LIFE

For you are the fountain of life, the light by which we see.
—Psalm 36:9 NLT

I stood with a group of twenty college students in the center of campus underneath a palm tree. A few feet away from us stood Janelle, one hand holding her phone and the other plugging her one ear so she could drown out the noise around her. We were in the middle of an outreach on a college campus in central California, and we all knew that Janelle's mom was sick with cancer. An urgent phone call could not be good news.

She returned to the group and let us all know that she had just been told that her mom was dying. She said to us, "My mom is not going to experience healing here but complete healing in heaven." I remember thinking, "I could never be as brave or articulate as her." I didn't know yet that I would be standing in her shoes just a few years later. I know now that people who suffer are not better or wiser than anyone else, they are simply doing the best they can with the grace God gives them in the moment. I couldn't picture myself responding to tragedy with wisdom and grace because I hadn't experienced it yet. God knew what the future held, even if I didn't.

After Janelle shared her the news of her phone call, we huddled in closer and prayed over her and for her family. She was no longer separate, disconnected, or alone with the heavy burden of fatal news. She was in the center of our huddle, surrounded and strengthened by our prayers. Grievers should never be ostracized or put on a spiritual pedestal but encircled by prayers and kindness. Just because we cannot fully understand someone's grief doesn't mean we can't draw them close.

Later that day, we were paired up to go around campus and start conversations with strangers about faith. As we were trying to decide who to pair up with, I was thinking about fountains and how I would like to go find one on campus and sit next to it. As I was thinking this, Janelle shared she was going to find a fountain. "I think I'm supposed to go with you," I told her. Sure enough, in the middle of campus, next to a square brick lecture hall was a small stone fountain with concrete seating all around, just like the one I had been daydreaming about earlier. We didn't strike up very many conversations with people, instead we spent some time praying and talking about Janelle's mom. By the time we returned to the group, my fingers were damp with mist from sitting at the fountain's edge.

I remember Janelle's strength, her bravery, and also her grief from that day. When I found myself, three years later, receiving that same dreaded call telling me my mom was really, truly, dying, I found Janelle's audacious words returning to me: "My mom is going to experience complete healing in heaven." The words filled me with comfort as I struggled to understand what was happening to my family. I didn't feel as wise or articulate as Janelle at that moment, but God lent me her words to use as my own. He was sitting with me and Janelle at the fountain that day, and he was sitting with me the day I got the phone call that my mom was dying.

In Jesus's presence, those whom we lose and those who remain on earth can be made whole through faith. In the darkness of death and decay, his life lights our way to the Father. And when we find the Father, we find the fountain—the fountain of faith that we can return to again and again in our grief as we grapple with our own unimaginable tragedy.

Dear God, you knew what was coming next in my life,
even if I didn't.

I couldn't see myself facing this type of grief,
yet here I am, and you remain at my side.

You were already giving the words of comfort
I would need.

Thank you for the people who surround me in prayer.

Thanks for being the fountain of faith that never runs
dry. Amen.

DAY 42

HOPE CALLS MY NAME

Now the LORD came and stood and called as at other times, "Samuel! Samuel!" And Samuel answered, "Speak, for Your servant hears." Then the LORD said to Samuel: "Behold, I will do something in Israel at which both ears of everyone who hears it will tingle." —1 Samuel 3:10–11 NKJV

Katrina!" my mom yelled out while in the women's bathroom at a minor league baseball game, trying to locate me in the crowded line. The concrete walls echoed my name across the stalls like a curse. It was 2005, and Hurricane Katrina had recently devastated New Orleans. Suddenly, my name was not my own. As a middle schooler, I felt like everyone was looking at me, thinking, "What an unfortunate name!" Have you ever felt like everyone is looking at you after tragedy has struck? Your name is forgotten and instead you wear a different label such as: Widower, Orphan, Fatherless, Only Child; these titles can feel like unwanted nametags we can't remove.

After my mom died, I hated the "motherless daughter" label I felt like I had stuck to my shirt. When I went to church, I felt the same middle-school self-consciousness rise up in me as I imagined people's pitying looks cast in my direction. In my mind, I wasn't just "Katrina" anymore; I was "Katrina-who-lost-her-mom." I daydreamed about moving to a new town and not telling anyone about what happened. More than anything, I just wanted to hear my mom say my name again. It didn't matter if it was the "Katrina Jean!" she would call me when I was in trouble or the more affectionate "Trina." I would've taken anything. I saved a voicemail from her so I could replay it over and over again to hear the recorded version of her saying my name. I needed to have some hope again that I would hear a beloved voice call out my name.

When I felt like everyone around me saw me as only a grieving person, I remembered the story of Samuel hearing God's voice calling his name. He served under the high priest Eli in the temple of the Lord. He wasn't being raised in the home of his mother but in the house of the Lord. One night, Samuel hears a voice in the night call out: "Samuel! Samuel!" Samuel feels confused and thinks Eli is calling for him. After three times of running into Eli's room, Eli finally figures out that it's probably God who is calling Samuel's name. He tells Samuel that the next time God calls his name he should respond with: "I'm listening, Lord. What do you want me to do?" (1 Samuel 3:9 CEV). Samuel does just that, and God gives him a terrible message for Eli about the consequences coming for Eli's rebellious sons. Everything God told Samuel comes true, and this is just the first instance of God talking directly to Samuel throughout his life.

The story of Samuel hearing God calling his name in the night stuck to me like glue when I heard it as a young child. "How would

I respond if I heard God call my name?" I wondered to myself. I thought it was so personal that God started the conversation by saying Samuel's name. It always struck me as being so direct and familiar. One night, as I lay sleeping, I had a dream that God called out to me: "Trina." I thought that maybe I had made it up, but I couldn't shake the feeling of love and acceptance I felt in that dream. It wasn't an audible voice like Samuel heard, but it filled me with hope at a time when I needed to hear my name called out in love.

Even though you will always miss your loved one's voice, God is calling out your name, if you will only listen to him. He is a voice of hope during the dark nights.

Dear Jesus, here I am.

I'm listening.

What do you want me to do?

You call out my name, and it's a voice of love and hope.

Even though it feels right now like I will always be viewed as a griever, you see me as your beloved. Amen.

DAY 43

LOVE CALLS US TO SERVE ONE ANOTHER

A new commandment I give to you, that you love one another: just as I have loved you, you also are to love one another. By this all people will know that you are my disciples, if you have love for one another. —John 13:34–35 ESV

I took a deep breath as I walked across the well-lit church lobby and approached the sanctuary doors. Before I could take a step farther, my friend Shirley pulled me into a hug in the doorway. "I know how hard it can be the first time coming back to church after you lose somebody." She was one of my mom's oldest friends and like a second mom to me. She looked at me with kind eyes, and in that moment, I felt seen. Shirley had laid aside her own grief for my mom in order to recognize mine. Sacrificial love like this reminds me that church is so much more than a building or a place to be entertained. It's an opportunity to show Christ's love and encourage one another. It's a gathering place where we can be encouraged and invite others in.

Jesus gave us the perfect picture of what sacrificial love looks like during his last days on earth. The day before he died, he broke bread and drank wine with his disciples for the traditional Passover meal. Jesus knew he was going to die soon, but he put aside his own fear and grief during that meal and focused on caring for his disciples so that they would be ready for what came next. At that table sat one disciple whom he knew would betray him for thirty pieces of silver. Also at that table was John, who is described as the disciple "whom Jesus loved" (John 13:23 ESV). I imagine Jesus looking each one of them in the eye as he explained how his body and blood, which would be sacrificed for them, were represented by the wine and bread they were consuming. Before he was arrested, he urged them to "love one another just as I have loved you" (John 13:34 ESV). Even as he faced death, his last words to them were reminding them to love each other.

Going back to church that day wasn't easy, but because of Shirley's kindness, I made it through the front door. This made it a little easier to cross that threshold the next Sunday and the Sunday after that. Going to church and letting myself be seen by other people was still challenging. One time I started crying during an emotional vocal performance, and Jesse took me home early. Another time, none of my close friends were there, so I sat in the back row trying to blend into the chairs around me. I was showing up consistently, but inside I was beginning to question my place there: Why am I here? What's the point?

One Sunday, as I entered the lobby, one of the pastors pulled me aside and asked, "Will you help serve communion today?" Internally, I panicked: "Me? No, I'm the last person who should do this." But I felt a tug on my heart that said it was time for me to serve again. "Sure," I said, taking the slip of paper she handed me. As I unfolded it, I read the words: "Christ's body broken for you." As the line of friends and strangers came through, I repeated this truth over and over again, as they tore off tiny pieces of the bread. Looking each person in the eye, I realized that each and every one of the people before me had their own joys and sorrows, just like me. I realized that it might be hard for some of them to be here too. I discovered at that moment that I wanted to find those people, greet them at the door, and say, "I know how hard it is to come back to church." It was time to show Christ's sacrificial love to other people like me.

Dear Jesus, help me as I navigate returning to church after being away for a time.

It's hard to put myself back in a vulnerable space with other people.

Thank you for friends who encourage me and remind me that you love me and sacrificed yourself for me. Amen.

DAY 44

REMAIN BRAVE AS YOU WAIT FOR HEAVEN

But our citizenship is in heaven, and from it we await a Savior, the Lord Jesus Christ, who will transform our lowly body to be like his glorious body, by the power that enables him even to subject all things to himself. —Philippians 3:20–21 ESV

When my mom was sick, her dear friend Jamie gave her a little canvas that stood up on a small easel. It was painted turquoise with a heart at the center, and it said, "Brave One," in bold lettering. My mom displayed it near her recliner so she could see it every day. I often caught a rare smile from her when she looked at it. I imagine that she heard her friend Jamie saying, "Hey, brave lady!" when she looked at it. It's hard to feel brave when you're suffering. Depression? Bargaining? Denial? All of those. But bravery, like beauty, is in the eye of the beholder. We are often so close to our own stories that it can be tough to recognize our own bravery. Sometimes bravery simply looks like getting up in the morning.

The week before my mom's memorial service, Jamie found herself picking the abundant blueberry crop in her backyard. She told me she was wondering, "Shelly, are you picking blueberries too? What new things have you discovered in heaven? I can't wait to find out." I imagine her fingers were stained indigo as she stared up at the sky that day, contemplating her brave friend exploring heaven ahead of her. When I think of grieving, I often picture Jamie picking blueberries and missing her dear friend. It makes me feel less alone to know that other people miss her too when they pick blueberries, wash dishes, or drive home from work. I am not the only one wondering what heaven is really like and what my mother might be doing up there.

Maybe she is leading heavenly language classes, blessing babies, or berry picking in vast orchards. I have no idea. Jesus always saw and nurtured that brave spark within my mother during her time on earth. I imagine that spark is the size of a bonfire now. Heaven is a great mystery to me. I've had loved ones die who didn't follow Jesus. I don't know if they reached out to God in their final moments or not, but I hope they did. I pray for peace if you too are wrestling with questions about your loved one's final destination. God is just and faithful and offers us countless chances to choose him every day.

It takes a certain kind of bravery to live on this earth, where heaven is still a great mystery and we pick the meager fruits of our labor. My dad often said, "This earth is not my home!" which I would respond to with an eye roll as a teenager. But I know now that he is right: we are citizens of heaven who are waiting for the day that God will change our earthly bodies and make everything new (Philippians 3:20). Yet, for the present time, there are still blueberry bushes to pick, carpool lines to wait in, and new sorrows that arise. It can feel so mundane, ordinary, and even meaningless at times.

My friend Kamille once quoted Ecclesiastes to me, which says, "There is nothing new under the sun" (1:9 NIV). Kamille told me that she hopes in God because "he is above the sun." God has a view far above our own and can see the greater scope of what is really happening. God is above the earth he has hand-painted. He sees the whole masterpiece of our lives, and one day, he will transform our earthly bodies into heavenly ones. God calls us to be filled with wonder about heaven, even as the weight of grief on earth feels heavy.

Dear God, I sometimes wonder what heaven will be like and what those who have died do there.

Help me to be brave, living in this world without my loved one.

I miss them every day, and I know other people do too.

My grief can feel overwhelming and meaningless some days, so please help me to be brave.

There is nothing under this sun you don't already know, so please give me the perspective I need. Amen.

DAY 45

REMAIN A SIGNATURE OF GOD'S LOVE

Now it is God who establishes both us and you in Christ. He anointed us, placed His seal on us, and put His Spirit in our hearts as a pledge of what is to come.
—2 Corinthians 1:21–22 BSB

The necklace gleamed in my small and delicate hand—the hand formed from my mother's DNA. Etched in soft cursive on the back of the gold circle charm were the words "Love you, Mom." My sister had taken my mom's handwriting from a greeting card and ordered matching necklaces for both of us. She said to me, "I'm sorry if it's too much. I just wanted to give you something special." "No, it's perfect," I said as I watched my tears splash across its shiny surface. My sister and I wear our necklaces often, wearing the plain side out with the signature close to our hearts; the metal has now faded from gold to a tarnished bronze.

I wore my necklace to a women's retreat a year after my mom died. As I waited in line for carrot cake that first night, one of the ladies asked about it, intrigued by its faint, golden glimmer. I turned it around and showed the inscription of my mom's handwriting and explained how my sister had ordered it custom-made. A few tears rolled down her cheeks as I talked—some hidden grief awakened inside her. Maybe she was thinking of her own children. Maybe she was letting out sadness we don't create enough space for in our everyday lives. Either way, I knew that both of us were united as sufferers as I let her see inside my heart and my grief for a brief moment.

I love that necklace so much because it's one of the few sentimental mementos I have to remind me of my mom. She was not an especially sentimental person. She would make your favorite meal or gently tease you to show her love. As she grew sicker, she didn't have the emotional capacity to create mementos, and that wasn't her style anyway. So, when I want to remember her strength, I wear the necklace. When I want to remember her beauty, I wear it. When it matches my outfit, I wear it. I pray that, as I wear it, I will feel the Lord's peace wash over me in a new and powerful way that brings tears of healing and remembrance.

If you are crawling through the murky depths of grief today, keep going. If you're crying bittersweet tears of longing, keep going. If you're so mad you could scream, keep going. Just like we all have our own unique signatures, we all have our own unique experiences with grief. If we call Jesus our friend, we have his signature written on our hearts. He has called us his own forever.

*Dear Jesus, you have etched your name upon my heart
as a seal of love.*

*No matter what, my identity is in you, and you are
my source of healing.*

*Just as I clutch my memories with my loved one close,
I know that you draw me close to you. Amen.*

DAY 46

FAITH PARTS THE SEAS OF LIFE

When you pass through the waters, I will be with you; and when you go through the rivers, they will not overwhelm you. When you walk through the fire, you will not be scorched; the flames will not set you ablaze. —Isaiah 43:2 BSB

The Israelites had just left Egypt—the land where they had been enslaved. Pharaoh, the ruler of Egypt, initially let them leave his country. Then his heart hardened, and he changed his mind again. He chased them into the desert with all of his chariots and warriors. I imagine that the ground beneath the Israelites shook with the sound of horse hooves and warrior cries. Maybe it was even loud enough to drown out the sound of the waves ahead of them. An entire people group was on the verge of extermination, with their backs to a body of unpassable water. They were going to drown underneath these waves or be killed by the approaching Egyptians. Two options loomed ahead of them: fight or sink—give up or give in. Yet, with God there was a third option: "Then Moses raised his hand over the sea, and the Lord opened up a path through the water with a strong east wind. The wind blew all that night, turning the seabed into dry land" (Exodus 14:21 NLT).

They could rest all night and sleep because God was working on their behalf. Moses raised up his hand and a path started to form in the water. Even if the Egyptians attacked at the first rays of dawn, God would save them. This is not how this miraculous event has been depicted in pop culture. I thought it was one grand moment of dramatic waterworks, and then voilà! A path in the water! When in reality, God was blowing the waters of chaos apart throughout all the darkness of the night. The Israelites arose to the light of dawn to see their salvation—a clear view of the path God had created for them through the sea.

Are you going through a long, dark, night of the soul? A time of trial and questioning, with enemies on one side and insurmountable waters on the other? Maybe you feel trapped, like there's no way out. Why keep going? Why even believe in God anymore? What's the point? The doubts and lies are chasing you down. Give up or give in; fight or drown. Yet, in the midst of all your questions, remains a third option: rest. Rest in God's love as he creates a path for you.

As you endure the darkness, God is shifting the winds around you. He is creating a path through the waters. The enemy will not win or overtake you. You may not see it until that first break of dawn when light floods your vision again. Reach out your hand and ask for his power to show up.

Dear Jesus, part the waters and make a way through
for me to continue on your path of light
and wisdom.

Protect me from the deep waters of unresolved
depression, the hot flames of consuming anxiety,
and whatever troubles I may face today.
Amen.

DAY 47

THE HOPE FOUND AROUND US

The Lord is all I have, and so in him I put my hope.
—Lamentations 3:24 GNT

A year before my mom died, on a hot and starless summer night, I stood before a sign that lit up the city block with one simple word: "Hope." Dozens of Edison light bulbs made up the word, and the sign stood taller than me. As I stood before the Hope sign, I could hear the soft murmur of a small crowd gathered around paper bags. They scribbled heartfelt notes and then placed candles into the bags. Each luminaria, as the bags were called, represented a loved one affected by cancer. I hadn't lost anyone close to me with cancer yet. I thought I was *only* there to support my sister who had organized her company's booth at the Relay for Life event. I found myself holding back tears for people I had never met.

I was unknowingly collecting examples of hope and resilience before I needed them myself. When my mom got her diagnosis, I felt so alone. "Who loses their mom to cancer at twenty-three?" I thought to myself. Then I thought, "Probably someone who lit one of those luminaria." God was gentle in comforting me as my heart felt like it was breaking. I didn't need a generic statement about hope; I needed a clear memory of people lighting candles in memory of their loved ones.

I couldn't understand the spiritual concept of hope for many years until I tied it to a visual metaphor like the bright luminaria sent by the people below to float away into the darkness. Hope can feel like a generic idea that doesn't have any real meaning. Using something we can visually see or experience can help us anchor this complex spiritual concept in order to have a deeper understanding of it. Maybe there's something physical you can see around you that represents hope. Maybe it's the excited face of your dog when you get home. Or an unexpected rainbow on your commute. Or an athlete rising up to win the whole game after a devastating injury. I don't know what that might be for you, but I do know that pictures of God's hope can be found around us.

Dear God, you are all I have, so I put my hope in you.

I can feel lonely or hopeless sometimes in the face
of death, but I know you will bring me
the comfort I need.

You shine bright in the darkness of my loneliness.

Help me to see your resilience in the people
and things around me. Amen.

DAY 48

LOVE SHOWS GREAT KINDNESS

Return to your rest, O my soul, For the Lord has dealt bountifully with you. —Psalm 116:7 NASB

Each morning the bell would ring, alerting sleepy, young bodies that school was about to start. I would stand outside of my storage-closet-turned-office with a thermos of coffee that the lunch lady had filled for me, greeting each student as they walked by. The children would spill out across the hallway—their hair still wet from the shower and faces still creased from sleep. Their feet pounded across the linoleum halls, breaking the quiet lull of teachers and staff preparing carpeted rooms for learning. Another day had begun. Another opportunity for kindness, patience, and love.

I was working as an AmeriCorps volunteer, running and staffing a place in the elementary school called the Care Room. One of the teachers was inspired to create a safe space where kids could get extra support and attention, and I was tasked with bringing it to life. Each teacher had paper slips that students could use if they needed a break, extra homework help, or simply some extra kindness. They could come to the Care Room and get one-on-one attention. We had a high population of students without homes, living in poverty, or with extra challenges. Instead of waiting until kids acted out because of their high needs and sending them directly to the principal's office, they could come to my room instead and sit on the couch and have a listening ear. Or play with kinetic sand in silence. Or have a college student volunteer sit beside them and read their assignment aloud. I even had a mini-fridge stocked with extra cartons of milk and apples from the lunchroom. There was a fluffy couch, twinkly lights, and a large stuffed bear to hug if needed.

I remember one little first grader came into my room with a Care Room slip crumpled in his balled-up fists. He was shaking because he was so upset. I got down on his level and told him, "You can play with the toys on the table or take a seat wherever. I'm here if you want to talk." He nodded in response and sat in the child-sized rocker and started playing with some math manipulatives in front of him. Slowly, he shed his anger and looked up at me occasionally with bright eyes. You could see the pain floating away from him in waves as he sat in the room. About fifteen minutes later, he told me he was ready to go back, and he left the room happily whistling down the hallway. That room was magic, and I had to pinch myself sometimes to believe that I really had the privilege to run it.

It was no accident that this was my job when my mom had her cancer diagnosis. The school that I had poured my heart and soul into caring for, in turn, showed great kindness to me. The teachers asked after my mom and helped me out when I needed to miss work to visit her. I started out the job thinking that it was my responsibility to care for others visiting this room, and soon, I realized I was just as much in need of a Care Room as any of the kids who visited. Who doesn't need a safe space to process?

Do you believe that God cares for you? That you can come to him with your fists balled-up in anger and let his presence melt away your rage? It's no accident that you are reading this devotional right now. He will meet you in your current distress. He is the God of all comfort, waiting for us at the doors of our confusion and rage, ready to turn them into places of respite and refuge.

Dear Jesus, please provide the space and kindness
my soul longs for.

Let me rest in your love.

You have always dealt generously with me. Amen.

DAY 49

GRIEF IS ALWAYS CHANGING

The Lord *wraps himself in light as with a garment; he stretches out the heavens like a tent.* —Psalm 104:2 NIV

Grief isn't always linear or predictable, much like the weather in the Pacific Northwest. People here like to say, "Wear layers!" because one minute you have sunshine, the next it's a torrential downpour, and then there might be a few snow flurries with some hail mixed in. I constantly have to adjust the layers of clothing I wear to stay comfortable. Grief on different days can change just as quickly as rain to sun. It requires me to be adaptable and change in response to how I'm feeling. My grief will never completely go away because the love I have for my mom will never fade. I have to adjust my own expectations for myself in response to the ever-changing conditions grief gives me.

Some days, grief is like a blizzard, and I need a heavy winter coat to protect and comfort me. Other days, grief is only a light shower, and I can make it through with just a rain jacket. Sometimes I breeze through the days I expected grief to punch me in the stomach. Other times, days that should be "easy" are unexpectedly tough, like when I saw someone wearing the same black Costco coat my mom always wore. The lady had the same shoulder-length bob as my mom, and the resemblance knocked the air out of my lungs. All I could do was stare at her until my breath came back to me.

The day of my mom's memorial service, I wore a knee-length raincoat that used to be hers. The belted waist and metallic sheen of the coat felt like armor upon my bones as I watched the drizzly rain on the drive over to the church. It was like her memory was wrapped tightly around my waist, giving me the strength to hug friends with tight smiles and eyes red from crying. I thought the memorial service would knock me over, yet I was able to stand up front and read a poem I wrote for her about pumpkin pie, trees, and how she smelled like chamomile. The flood waters of grief were held back until a few days later.

Because my mom and I were around the same height, I inherited all of her old jackets. One day, I pulled out her purple raincoat, and as I reached my hands inside the pockets, I felt the softness of worn tissues. No matter what jacket she wore, she always carried tissues in all the pockets. As I held her folded tissue in my hand, the tears started to flow with no sign of stopping. It was a good thing I held those tissues in my hands because I was soon a snotty, wet mess. It felt like, even after she died, she was still trying to take care of me, still trying to wipe my tears away.

Like the layered clothes we wear outdoors, we have to adjust to the circumstances around us. But we don't have to bear this burden alone; we are enveloped in the presence of a God who clothes himself in light and calls the heavens his home. A few times, I've prayed in the midst of my worst grief: "God, can I get some relief?" and I have felt it lift off my shoulders for a moment. It doesn't always work this way, but we serve a God who never leaves us. He gave up his garments and died on the cross for us, so that we could be clothed in his righteousness. He took on shame, grief, and sin so that we could wear robes of royalty someday in heaven. His sacrifice should take our breath away.

Dear Lord, I don't always know what my grief
is going to look like on a day-to-day basis,
but you know.

Can I get some relief today?

Would you wrap me up in your light?

Your power and majesty are awe-inspiring. Amen.

DAY 50

BEYOND THE ASHES

To all who mourn in Israel, he will give a crown of beauty for ashes, a joyous blessing instead of mourning, festive praise instead of despair. In their righteousness, they will be like great oaks that the LORD has planted for his own glory.
—Isaiah 61:3 NLT

On my eighteenth birthday I was in a small village outside of Kraków, Poland, on a high-school mission trip. It was mid-April, and the wide, gray skies of the Polish countryside were punctuated with stark trees and dry grasses bent forward from the harsh winds of a lingering winter. My stomach was always full of warm kielbasa sausage and steaming mugs of sweet black tea during that trip. We were staying in the local mayor's house, which doubled as an inn when needed, and she had invited some of us ladies to a tea that day along with some of the local matriarchs of the town. One of my youth leaders told them it was my birthday, and when we arrived, the Polish ladies surprised me with a small cake decorated with delicate flower blossoms. One of the ladies handed me a bouquet of handmade paper red roses, each crisp and delicate in my fingers. I kept that bouquet of paper roses for years afterward until it faded to a dull pink and started to unravel.

In Eugene Peterson's paraphrase of Isaiah 61:3, he phrases this beautiful passage as "bouquets of roses instead of ashes, messages of joy instead of news of doom" (MSG). When I read that wording, I couldn't help but think of my paper rose bouquet from Poland. I longed for God to take the smoldering ashes of my losses and quickly trade them for roses. Yet, this verse is not just about me; it's addressed to Israel, a community of believers. It's about a gathering of people celebrating God renewing their city and their land. I picture grandmas who fold delicate paper layers into roses, young people eating slices of cake, and groups of people gathered around bonfires to roast sausages because the land is full of peace and everything has been made right by God. Grief can spread across a community, but redemption and healing can spread just as fast.

Later that day, as we painted the local school gym, our translator received an urgent call on her phone. We could hear her quietly weeping in the next room over. "What happened? Was her daughter alright?" we wondered to each other. When she returned, she shared with us that the president of Poland and his wife, along with ninety-four other people, including government officials, had all died in a plane crash that day. She shared how beloved her country and government were to her. Especially since Poland had a history of occupation, having their own government was a source of pride. This land that had opened its arms to me on my birthday was now one covered in mourning. One moment we were celebrating and eating cake, and the next we were praying together for their country. Their fragrant bouquet of joy and generosity were now marked with the ashes of tragedy.

What remains in the ashes of our grief? We often find ourselves holding both the bouquet of roses and the smoldering fires of loss at the same time. We grieve individually but also collectively. God's people longed to see their home, Zion, restored to its former glory. God promised them that one would come who would bring something even better; he was going to revive their country and bring everlasting joy. Jesus was the one; and his love remained in the ashes. It grew like tiny rosebud seeds underneath the scorched earth. His love remains in the present too.

A month later, I stood before my congregation as a part of Youth Sunday where I was one of a few invited to share about our trip. I brought with me the bouquet of paper roses and shared about the resiliency and strength of a people who had endured so much loss yet kept on fighting and believing. Five years later, I would hold a bouquet of crisp ferns and dark red roses as I exchanged wedding vows. Two months after my wedding, I would once again stand on that same stage and share a poem at my mother's memorial service. Ashes and roses. Celebration and mourning. News of doom transformed into messages of joy that will never fade and will not unravel.

Dear Jesus, you meet me in the stark fields of my grief
and the tender bouquets of comfort I receive.

I know that someday you "will give a crown of beauty
for ashes" (Isaiah 61:3 NLT).

You understand that grief can be not only personal
but experienced by a whole community.

Let your glory transform my mourning. Amen.

DAY 51

FAITH BELIEVES IN NEW MERCIES

The steadfast love of the Lord *never ceases;*
his mercies never come to an end; they are new every morning;
great is your faithfulness. —Lamentations 3:22–23 ESV

I love slow mornings where there is time to savor the moment and no rush off to work or responsibilities. Where I can witness the crisp morning air hitting the steam on my coffee mug as the sun peeks over the trees. Before my mom died, mornings like this seemed full of endless possibilities. But grief robbed me of this pleasure for a while. For a few months after my mom died, I would wake up and forget that she was dead. In those first few moments upon waking, the line between reality and heaven was blurred, and I would feel light and hopeful for the day. As the sunlight crept in, the truth that she was truly gone would shake me fully awake and sober me to the harshness of loss. Going to sleep at night meant that I would have to experience the loss and reawakening all over again. My blankets began to feel heavy, and my bedroom walls felt like they were closing in.

The mundane parts of my life persisted, even when my whole world had been turned upside down. There were tasks to be done and food to prepare. The toaster would pop up my bread, crisp and waiting to be buttered. The sun still came up, even when my mood was more suited toward a drizzling, endless grayness. The Bible my mom gave me sat on my bedside table, and if I'm honest, I wasn't sure if I had the spiritual strength to pick it up. "Where is God?" I would ask myself. "If his mercies are new every morning, why do they feel like they've been stolen from me?"

Before I lost my mom, I thought that being a Christian meant waking up every day with joy. God's daily mercies meant waking up to read my Bible, journal, and sit at Jesus's feet. Spending time in quiet contemplation with God is a wonderful start to the day, but it's not realistic to expect every day to go this way, especially when we are in the thickest part of grief. But his mercies are new even when I wake up with dread, depression, and no bread for the toaster. His mercies are new when my alarm keeps ringing, and I bury myself under the blankets. His mercies are new when I wake up from a nightmare where she's still sick, and I'm powerless to heal her. His mercies are new every morning because they are not dependent on me but on God's character. His faithfulness awakens the sun, not me. Thank goodness.

Those dark mornings where the loss hit me with such heaviness didn't mar God's faithfulness. In fact, they were an opportunity for the contrast of his mercy and truth to shine into my bedroom. As harsh as the memory of her death was to me, he was exceedingly gentle and gracious in turn. As Isaiah says, "Lord be gracious to us; we long for you. Be our strength every morning, our salvation in time of distress" (Isaiah 33:2 NIV). Sometimes my Bible was too heavy to open, so God would meet me in a song. Sometimes my nightmares were too much, and I would feel his presence in the grasp of my husband's palm as I held on to a tangible reminder of love. Sometimes I wouldn't feel anything at all, except for a longing for God's strength. Your mercies are new every day, God. No matter what.

Dear God, wake me up to your character
this morning—how your mercies and love
are unstoppable, persistent, and renewed each day.

Your mercies are new every morning, even when
I struggle to get out of bed.

Even when the darkness seems to take over.

I long for your strength to fill me today—the kind
that pierces through the darkness with light.
Amen.

DAY 52

HOPE TAKES REFUGE IN GOD

Be merciful to me, O God, be merciful to me, for in you my soul takes refuge; in the shadow of your wings I will take refuge, till the storms of destruction pass by. —Psalm 57:1 ESV

The exit signs flashed and stayed on. The flight attendant braced herself on the side of an aisle seat. The pilot's voice crackled over the loudspeaker explaining that we were experiencing turbulence as the plane attempted to land in the middle of an ice storm. My stomach did acrobatics as the plane dropped again and again. Dark storm clouds gathered outside the plane's narrow window without a single star above or patch of light below. I gripped Jesse's hand until my knuckles turned white. An audible "Woah!" could be heard when the turbulence continued and the sleeping passengers were jostled awake. I was uncertain and terrified yet tethered to the hopeful fact that the oxygen masks had not dropped. Planes always feel like strange places to me—somewhere between the destination I'm leaving and the place I'm going. I offered up a quick prayer to anchor me to heaven as I floated in the liminal space of the skies. I braced myself for a rough landing as we approached the runway ahead of us.

Isn't grief like this? It feels like a plane ride through an ice storm, where a rough landing seems almost guaranteed. There were, and still are, days where I am gripping tightly to my fear as the uncertainty of loss surrounds me. Grief feels like a flight I didn't sign up for, and one I would like to get off of. Yet my hope is tethered to the promise that God isn't overwhelmed by or anxious about my turbulent emotions. When I told my counselor about my flight anxiety, she told me to look at the flight attendants. She said, "If they're calm and acting like it's no big deal, you shouldn't worry either." Just like I needed to look to the flight attendants, I need to look to Jesus on the days when things in my life are unsteady. Is he panicking? No, he is sitting beside me, gripping my hand. Is he a muffled voice over the intercom making unseen promises of safety? No, he is the still, small voice that whispers encouragement in these times of uncertainty. God is the hope in the storm.

As the plane dipped onto the runway, I heard the comforting roar of wheels hitting the tarmac, and I said to Jesse, "Hello, beautiful ground! I'm never leaving you again!" As we exited the plane, the flight attendant told us it was raining outside so we should put on a jacket if we had one. As I stepped out onto the boarding stairs and felt the raindrops hit my face, I took a deep breath. My exhale came out in puffs as it hit the cold, wet air. I began to chuckle to myself, and soon Jesse did too. He asked me, "Why did we go with the cheap airline?" I replied, "Not worth the money saved," laughing harder now than before. As we walked indoors toward the baggage claim, I realized that I didn't want to just remember the fear, the anxiety, and the unknown. I wanted to remember the safe landings too.

Dear God, "In the shadow of your wings
I will take refuge, till the storms of destruction
pass by" (Psalm 57:1 ESV).

You are merciful to me on the days when my grief
feels turbulent and uncontrollable.

You grip my hand and stay close.

When I look at you, I'm reminded of what is right
and true.

In you my soul takes refuge. Amen.

DAY 53

WHEN EVERYTHING CHANGES

For you created my inmost being; you knit me together in my mother's womb. I praise you because I am fearfully and wonderfully made; your works are wonderful, I know that full well.
—Psalm 139:13–14 NIV

My life was a mess. Well, the map I had created of it, at least. A poster board lay before me covered in neon sticky notes marked with details like, "Going to college," "Dating Jesse," and other significant life events. Everyone on the leadership team I was a part of at church was supposed to create a "life map" as a reflective exercise to share with the group. Near the end of my arts-and-crafts project, I knocked over my mug and spilled hot coffee all over it. Rather than start over, I tried to salvage it and pretended that the stains were an intentional artistic effect. When I pulled it out to share with the group, my friends looked at it and asked, "What happened to your board?" I laughed it off and explained my mishap with the coffee, but inside I was in turmoil. "What is happening with my life?" I wondered.

Like the dark stains on my project, grief had tinted and changed every part of my life. After my mom died, I struggled to adjust to this new future I was living. What did my life look like without her steadying presence in it? Even small, mundane details, like emergency contacts, changed in response to her death. My friend Hannah experienced this after her sibling died and her family could all fit in one car again. The simple logistics of getting from one place to another change with a death in the family. Perhaps you can think of examples from your own life where things have changed.

I've heard it said that the only constant in life is change, which encourages me to put my faith in the unchangeable nature of God, who remains steady as everything else shifts around me. Three years after my mom died, I held my newborn niece for the first time. Her pink skin and curly hair were a wonder and miracle to behold. Our family was growing again, even as we were painfully aware of my mom's absence. I cheered for my brother as he walked across the stage to get his college diploma. I faced the exciting and scary decision to move out of state so my husband could attend his dream graduate school. Change, even in response to happy events, can still be stressful. I felt like a tangled mess of emotions, but God didn't see me that way.

Grief still affected every part of my life, but it could not stop new memories from forming. My niece had accomplished little besides crying and breathing in the moments since her birth, yet she was so beloved already. She didn't need to accomplish or prove anything to earn my family's adoration. She didn't fix or replace our grief, but rather she gave all of us a new opportunity to pour out our love and devotion. When I held my niece, I realized that God extends so much love toward me too.

Before you were born, God already loved you. Before anything had happened in your life, he knew everything that would come to be. He knitted you together in your mother's womb, and you are "fearfully and wonderfully made." You don't have to earn it or prove anything. No matter what happened to you, or how grief changed your life, God's love remains on you, his child.

Dear Jesus, my life can feel like such a mess sometimes.

I miss my loved one so much, especially when their absence is so apparent.

You created me and know every part of my life.

You loved me before I accomplished anything.

Your love was the first thing I knew
and nothing can take that away.
Amen.

DAY 54

DRIVING WITH "GRIEF BRAIN"

The Lord wraps himself in light as with a garment; he stretches out the heavens like a tent and lays the beams of his upper chambers on their waters. He makes the clouds his chariot and rides on the wings of the wind.
—Psalm 104:2–3 NIV

The bright lights of the police car flashed in my rearview mirror as I pulled over to the side of the road. My hands were shaking, and my heart was pounding. My husband was asleep in the passenger seat, and I gently nudged him awake. "I'm getting pulled over!" I said in a panic. "Why this place? Anywhere but here, God," I thought. This stretch of highway was the last place I had driven with my mom before she died. While we were driving, my mom had a seizure because of the tumor in her brain. My brother and I pulled over at the gas station on the side of the road to take care of her. After that seizure, I felt like she never truly came back. That night, as I drove the same road again, I felt numb and disoriented. As the state patrolman chastised me for driving in the fast lane with no cars to pass, I dutifully nodded in response. It felt like I was watching myself from far away as I felt pulled between two moments. My mind and body were reliving the day my mom had a seizure.

My head and heart were working hard to process the emotional baggage of that day. Just like I was coasting on cruise control when I should have moved over miles ago, my body and spirit were drifting on autopilot. I thought I was doing fine, until the police car lights lit up my back window. I've heard this brain fog referred to as "grief brain."[3] It's when your mind feels muddled and slow in response to grief for a period of time. My brain and body were on a new journey of grief, which requires a vast amount of energy. As I rolled up the window, relieved to only get a warning that night, I breathed a deep sigh of relief. "Can you drive the rest of the way?" I asked Jesse, and he happily obliged.

God doesn't work in spite of my "grief brain" but in partnership with it. He uses my weaknesses to alert me to his presence and my need for him. When my mind feels cloudy, my hands shake, and memories flood my brain, he is there. I'm grateful now that I was pulled over that night because I needed someone to interrupt me and make me pause. I needed to wake up to the toll grief was taking on my mind. Rather than fight my grief or beat myself up, it was OK to ask Jesse to take a turn driving so I could rest. A couple hours later, we arrived at our vacation rental in the heart of Portland, Oregan. I woke up to discover sunlit views of a lush rose garden across the street. I grabbed a steaming mug of coffee and curled up on the couch. God isn't only concerned

3. Traci Pedersen, "What Does Grief Do to Your Brain?" https://psychcentral.com/lib/your-health-and-grief.

with our final destination; he cares about the journey it takes us to get there too.

Dear Jesus, be present in those moments
when my brain is overwhelmed with grief.

You go before me and know what is coming next.

You stay beside me when I relive painful memories.

My weaknesses are not failures but rather reminders
of how much I need you. Amen.

DAY 55

REMAIN READY FOR WHAT'S NEXT

Rejoice greatly, O daughter of Zion! Shout aloud, O daughter of Jerusalem! Behold, your king is coming to you; righteous and having salvation is he, humble and mounted on a donkey, on a colt, the foal of a donkey. —Zechariah 9:9 ESV

My family and I were decked out in shades of bright green and royal blue, standing under the broad shadow of the sports stadium on a gray Seattle day. My dad played soccer throughout high school and college and loved to have us join him to watch a soccer match. Per tradition, we ate greasy hot dogs and marched with the parade led by the pep band a few blocks from the stadium. The air hummed with anticipation as we listened to the band before we made our way to the nosebleed section. The game was about to start! In the crowd, my dad recognized an old college buddy of his. "How's Shelly doing?" the friend asked my dad, and it was as if the music had stopped playing. The sky seemed to grow dimmer. Everything paused for us. "Oh no," I thought. "He doesn't know my mom died."

Nobody warned me how awkward grief can be. Every interaction in that first year became a juggling match. When running into people who knew my family, I used to wonder, "Do they know? If they don't know, do I tell them? If they do know, do I bring it up?" Grief changed the landscape of human interaction for me. As an introvert, social situations already took a lot of energy for me, and grief added extra burdens. It was exhausting to balance taking care of myself, educating people on what had happened, and letting them know how I was doing. I wanted to start writing the next chapter of my life, and it felt like every conversation had the potential to pull me backward into the past.

That day, marching with the soccer parade, reminded me of when Jesus rode into Jerusalem on a donkey. It was a festive and celebratory time, taking place during the Jewish holiday of Passover. Jesus came riding on a donkey, and people laid down their cloaks and declared him king. It echoed the parades of the Roman kings returning from battle in victory, except with Jesus it was different.[4] He wasn't on a mighty white steed but a humble donkey. There were no captors of war or battle spoils. The people did not know it yet, but Jesus was going to his death. It was a victory parade before the battle would be fought against death. Jesus already knew the outcome. Some of the same people who declared him king would soon turn against him and cry, "Crucify him!" Jesus's humility and sacrifice that day gave me comfort as I navigated the intricacies of grief.

Jesus led the victory parade that would eventually lead to his own death. He could have made it a great show of his power, but instead, he chose a humble and poignant path to separate himself

4. Max Harris, *Christ on a Donkey: Palm Sunday, Triumphal Entries, and Blasphemous Pageants* (Yorkshire, UK: ARC Humanities Press, 2019).

from the conquerors of the day. He came to save the very people who would try to kill him. If he can show great love like that, we can follow him. Our grief doesn't take away from the victory of Jesus's great love. In fact, it means we have access to his strength and his guidance. The next time someone asks, "How's your loved one doing?" we can stumble our way through without judgment toward ourselves. This is a hard thing we are learning how to do, and Jesus's humble example reminds us to keep going.

Dear God, you greet me with love whether I'm in
the middle of a victory parade or a funeral march.

You are righteous and full of salvation, even for those
who would later betray you.

Give me grace for myself and others as I figure out
how to talk about my loss and my grief.

You are the all-powerful God who humbled himself
for me.

Thank you. Amen.

DAY 56

FAITH IN A PERSONAL GOD

Are not five sparrows sold for two pennies? Yet not one of them is forgotten by God. Indeed, the very hairs of your head are all numbered. Don't be afraid; you are worth more than many sparrows. —Luke 12:6–7 NIV

As a child, my parents told me, "God knows the number of hairs on your head." I used to grasp individual strands of my hair between my fingers and count them, one by one, just to see how high I could count. Eventually, I would give up and move on to the next toy or activity, wondering, "How does God have the time for this?" When my mom was undergoing her first round of chemo and her hair started to fall out, one of my aunts offered to shave it off for her so she wouldn't have to deal with patchiness anymore, and I helped when the time came. "God surely has time for this—to witness every strand of my mom's hair being shaved off," I thought, as if challenging God to prove he really was who he said he was. "If you took the time to witness every strand of hair when it grew, won't you be there to tend to its loss?" I said to him, as I handed off scissors and wiped strands from my mom's neck.

Growing up, visits to my aunt's house meant free haircuts for us kids. She would wrap a bath towel around my shoulders, and I would watch as clumps of my hair fell to the linoleum floor. My aunt showed the same care and precision when caring for my mom that day. I did not count every hair that fell to the ground, but God did. Even though I challenged him to prove his character, I still saw his love in the careful movements of my aunt. Every snip from my aunt's scissors seemed to cut away another piece of uncertainty growing in my heart toward God. He was there amid our grief.

Perhaps you've experienced some hair loss in the course of your life. My first experience was about three months after my mom died. I told my hairdresser about my hair falling out as she trimmed my bangs, and she explained to me that hair loss is pretty common about three months after a stressful event. Watching strands of my hair collect in my shower drain left me feeling like part of me was getting washed away. "Really grief?" I thought to myself. "Can't I at least keep my hair?"

God knows me down to the most uncountable details, including each strand of hair on my head. He created me, from my fine hair to my thumb that juts backward. Nothing is missing or miscounted in his care. Eventually my hair grew back, and I dyed it bright red because I had always been curious what it would look like. My new shade didn't fix anything or cover up the tufts of new growth on the top of my scalp, but it felt good to do something different. Some days there is so much I fear and cannot control, and I imagine that God says to me, "I have more than enough time for this."

Dear God, you count every hair upon my head,
and no small joy or deep sorrow goes unwitnessed by you.

Do not forget me.

Don't turn your back on my grief.

I need you. Amen.

DAY 57

HOPE IN GOD'S WORD

So the Word became human and made his home among us. He was full of unfailing love and faithfulness. And we have seen his glory, the glory of the Father's one and only Son.
—John 1:14 NLT

My feet crunched the dead leaves as we wound our way along the circular path of Lake Padden. Giant trees loomed over the trail, enclosing us and opening back up again to offer views of the small, sparkling body of water. My friend Sarah and I were chatting about our lives, and she asked me, "What have you been reading in the Bible lately?"

I slowed my pace and told her, "Actually, I haven't been able to read much since my mom died. It's been too overwhelming." I hadn't told very many people this because I wasn't sure I could explain why. Before my mom died, I would read my Bible every morning and journal several pages in response. I would sit in the soft corner of the couch with a steaming mug of coffee with a large dollop of cream, fancy pens in hand. This comforting routine served as an anchor. Yet here I was, as a griever, unable to crack open a Bible for more than a minute or two. I would read a verse and then break into sobs. That's all I could handle.

Maybe you've never picked up a Bible before. Or maybe your Bible is covered in colored pencil sketches and the binding is falling apart in pieces from so much use. Maybe you read verses on a screen every day, or you find yourself, like me, unable to take in large portions of Scripture. Where do you go from here? What does reading the Bible look like for you in the midst of grief? Jesus was someone who valued connection, truth, and grace. When his students asked him how to pray, he kept it simple by laying out a short prayer they could use. Perhaps our posture toward the Bible should be similar: no need for anything fancy or overwhelming. Maybe for you, right now, that looks like five minutes in a psalm each day. Or maybe you are in a place where you can immerse yourself in whole chapters or books at a time. Or maybe, the single verse at the beginning of these devotionals. Know this: our value to God is not dependent upon our spiritual performance.

That day at the lake, after I shared my confession of little to no Bible reading, my friend Sarah had a look of surprise on her face. She had lived with me in the past and knew about my morning Bible routine. She made a quick recovery and didn't accuse or chastise me. She simply nodded and said, "That makes sense." Turns out that Sarah had been mentoring a college student who was also grieving the loss of her mom, and Sarah was beginning to learn the complexities of grief.

We stopped at the next bench and sat for a moment, looking at the lake and the glass-like ripples across its surface. A turtle poked its head out and climbed onto a log. I laughed and pointed it out. Then it hit me—the reason I could only read a verse at a time. It was because it hurt to remember who I was before my mom died. My faith was changing, evolving into something new and different in response to grief, and so, of course my relationship to the Bible looked different. Like that little turtle poking its head out of the water, I was emerging into a new space. Yet, new and different didn't have to be scary and alone. Jesus, the Word, came to dwell among us because he loved us. Having hope in Jesus means never being truly alone.

I turned my head and asked my friend, "Ready to keep walking?"

Dear God, be my constant companion
as my faith changes.

You are "full of unfailing love and faithfulness,"
and when I read the Bible, I get to learn more
about you.

Walk beside me on this path of dark waters
and unknown trails.

Guide me as I relearn how to approach the Bible
and encourage me to not give up.
Amen.

DAY 58

LOVE BRINGS US TOGETHER

By yourself you're unprotected. With a friend you can face the worst. Can you round up a third? A three-stranded rope isn't easily snapped. —Ecclesiastes 4:12 MSG

After feasting on BBQ chicken wings and cold lemonade, my siblings and I piled into my car. In the warmth of early May, we rolled down the windows and rock songs by America flowed around us as the wind whipped through our hair. Our mom was dying, but at that moment, you would never know. We were simply three siblings in their twenties, escaping to the nearby chain eatery with its dark booths, happy hour specials, and no scent of sickness. We had to get out of the house that smelled of bleach spray, sadness, and reheated cheese casseroles. Later that afternoon, one of us would probably hold back my mother's hair as the chemo treatments made her sick. Another would drop by the grocery store for meds and snacks. And the other might offer up tentative jokes, hoping for a response.

We were not meant to be alone or to carry our heavy burdens on our own. We need one another, for the warm meals and laughter, and for solidarity in caring for a dying parent. Even if it felt like everyone else had forgotten about us, for a brief moment, we felt carefree, light, and unbroken. We were, and are, a strand of three not easily broken—a handmade rope woven together through shared history, jokes, and tragedy. We are not perfect—not even close—but we are together.

There is nothing magical about the number three, but there is a practicality to it. Solely relying on one person to fulfill all of your needs can plant seeds of resentment or codependency, and so I highly recommended the number three. God himself operates within a trinity of God the Father, the Son, and the Holy Spirit: "For there are three that bear witness in heaven: the Father, the Word, and the Holy Spirit; and these three are one" (1 John 5:7 NKJV). They are all the same person and distinct at the same time, working together for God's purposes. It's a very complex topic that I can only begin to scratch the surface of, yet I think it's beautiful that God demonstrates how to operate relationally within his own dynamic being.

How can you reach out today and find someone to help alleviate the heaviness of sorrow? What lies are stopping you from reaching out? How could your entire day be transformed by the presence of another person who "gets it"? Perhaps there's a local grief group, such as GriefShare, you could join. Or maybe there's someone in your church who has also lost a parent recently who you could take a walk with. Maybe you should reach out to a family member who is also grieving and share a favorite beverage together. I hope that you find connection and camaraderie during what can be a lonely and isolating time.

Dear Jesus, thank you for first displaying what relationships should be like through the dynamic of the Trinity.

I'm learning that "with a friend you can face the worst" (Ecclesiastes 4:12 MSG).

Help me to recognize those who could help bear my burdens with me. Amen.

DAY 59

REMAIN CONNECTED TO OTHERS

A generous person will prosper; whoever refreshes others will be refreshed. —Proverbs 11:25 NIV

"I need to make a phone call I've been putting off," my mom told me as she picked up her phone. I gave her a puzzled look in response, curious about who she was calling. I eavesdropped as she discussed school events and beloved students. She asked for prayer for her cancer and thanked the person on the other end. "What was that about?" I asked after she hung up. "Closure," she told me and explained it was a coworker from the school she used to work at. My mom had entered a toxic working environment a few years prior where two of the staff had been involved in an illicit affair on school grounds. The gossip and drama that ensued became such a problem that professional mediators had to be brought in. As a new employee, there was little welcome or support for my mom. She tried her best to stay out of the conflict, but it was hard to see her lose the joy and enthusiasm she usually brought to her classes. I was surprised she would contact any of her former coworkers.

I was convicted that day to reflect on the relationships in my own life. Were there people I was holding grudges against? Would I have the courage to obey God if he asked me to call someone? My mom was given six months to live, but in reality, it was only four. There wasn't enough time to resolve every relationship in her life, but God reminded her of that one coworker at that moment. It's so easy for me to forget how temporary life is and that nobody knows how much time they have left. Death forces me to ask hard questions I might have otherwise ignored.

I was angry at first that some of my mom's last years teaching were so difficult. But in the last year before her diagnosis, she accepted a teaching position at a school down the road from her parents' home. It was a long commute for my mom, so she spent a lot of time with my grandparents. My grandpa would make her peanut butter toast for breakfast, and my grandma would prepare the guest room for her the nights she needed to sleep over. My grandpa, a high school dropout, marveled at his daughter's classroom filled with whiteboards of Spanish verb conjugations and mementos from her travels abroad. My mom would not have spent that precious time with her parents if her previous job had not been so difficult. The time we spend with people is not an accident.

God puts people in our lives at different times for different purposes. We need his discernment about when it's appropriate to reach out and when it's time to walk away. Sometimes that means making a phone call to get closure. Sometimes it means taking an inconvenient job to be conveniently close to someone. We don't have to find a reason for everything in our lives but, rather, be ready for opportunities to love people. It's much easier to ignore other people, but God does not ignore us.

Dear God, the time I spend with other people is no accident, and I need your help to love others well.

Losing someone makes me reevaluate the relationships I have.

Is there someone I need to reach out to and call?

Is there a change I need to make to be closer to someone?

Guide me today and help me out. Amen.

DAY 60

REMAIN INTEGRATED IN THE HOLY SPIRIT

You keep track of all my sorrows. You have collected all my tears in your bottle. You have recorded each one in your book. —Psalm 56:8 NLT

I sat beneath the sweeping emerald trees under gray skies. A rolling field stretched before me at a small park between streets of craftsman-style homes near my rental. Our four-hundred-square-foot tiny house, with our refrigerator in the bedroom, had been making me feel claustrophobic, and I had needed to get outside. I watched a group of forty-something intramural rugby players finish their practice and then scatter to their individual cars. The one person playing fetch with their dog trotted back home. There I remained, with my red eyes finally freeing the tears I had been holding back for too long. "Grief makes you cry, so why not cry under a beautiful tree?" I thought to myself.

Like the great leader of Israel, Deborah, I set up my court underneath that tree to meet God and have my disputes with him resolved: "She held court under the Palm of Deborah between Ramah and Bethel in the hill country of Ephraim, and the Israelites went up to her to have their disputes decided" (Judges 4:5 NIV). God often meets me underneath trees. Something about getting away from stale indoor air and the busyness of tasks clears my mind.

It's easier to find God in the places where we are quiet and listen. Perhaps that is in the car, on a run, or while chopping vegetables for dinner. We all need safe places to converse with the Holy Spirit—places to set up camp and cry a little if needed or to simply collect our thoughts. You have come so far already—sixty days of taking the time to meet God here in these pages and to settle the rumblings in your spirit where they are disturbed.

It is good to lean on other people in times of trouble, but there is always an inherent loneliness to grief. Even a brother, parent, or friend cannot fully understand the unique relationship you've lost when a loved one dies. Only you and that person knew all the funny things you did together, like the time you made up costumes from winter gear in the trunk of your car to trick-or-treat in middle school. Not only are you grieving the loss of your person, but of all the secret handshakes, inside jokes, and beloved memories the two of you shared. Grief is experienced as a group but also on the individual level.

When my mom died, my dad was grieving the loss of his spouse of over thirty years. His day-to-day reality was forever altered. My brother still had college courses to complete and lived in the same town as my parents. He ended up moving back in with my dad for a time and taking a year off from college running. My sister and I were farther away, so our day-to-day life didn't change as much, however we were still very much affected. My sister felt the pressure as the oldest daughter to be the matriarch of the family. She was also newly married and beginning to form her own family. I was beginning my teaching career and didn't have my mom to guide or mentor me anymore. I was also the "peacekeeper" of my family as the middle sibling and struggled to try to pull us together as we each tried to individually work through our grief. Each one of us faced a different reality in response to the absence of my mom.

My brother went for long runs in the rain and leaned on his best friends on his worst days. My sister tried out new hobbies and excelled at her job. I pivoted away from teaching jobs and went for walks in the park. My dad sipped coffee on the back porch like he always had and called up his buddies from college. God met each one of us wherever and however we chose to grieve. That day, when I cried beneath the tree, it began to rain softly. The thick branches and leaves of the tree above me protected me from the drops. God spoke to me that day and reminded me that he is the one to "keep track of all my sorrows" and that he "collected all my tears" in his bottle (Psalm 56:8 NLT). Even if my grief looks and expresses itself differently than other people's, God will always be there to count each and every tear.

Dear Jesus, no one can fully understand the grief I'm experiencing, and that can be lonely sometimes.

Help me to get out in nature so that I can give myself space to cry and talk to you.

You witness my moments of sorrow no matter where I find myself.

You count every single one of my tears, and someday soon, you will wipe them away forever.
Amen.

PART 3

THE GREATEST OF THESE IS LOVE

God's love encapsulates the eternal nature of faith, hope, and love being put into action in us and through us. Grief will be with us for our whole lives, but God remains with us no matter what.

DAY 61

FAITH REACHES NEW HEIGHTS

And without faith it is impossible to please him, for whoever would draw near to God must believe that he exists and that he rewards those who seek him. —Hebrews 11:6 ESV

My hands were itching as I held on to the braided rope. My heart was pounding as adrenaline pumped through my veins. The smell of chalk mixed with sweat and a side of disinfectant filled my nostrils. I looked up at the exposed rafters of the warehouse that had been converted into a gym, and endorphins flooded my entire body. I grinned so wide it hurt my face.

"Jesse! Jesse! I did it!" I yelled at my husband who was deadlifting on the ground far below me, as I clung to the top of the rope, thirty feet above. I had finally climbed the rope and made it (almost) to the top. I had been working all morning to be able to even get off the ground, let alone make progress upward.

My first few attempts consisted of me climbing a couple of feet up and falling backward onto the mat. "Impossible," I thought. My trainer explained to me that climbing the rope wasn't just about upper body strength but also anchoring your feet on the rope as you moved up. By providing an anchor for the rest of my bodyweight to rest on, I could lift myself up by simply wrapping my feet together around the rope. Once I had the right technique, I found myself going a body length or two upward at a time, ignoring the fireman on the rope beside me who was going up one-handed. "I'm doing it!" I thought to myself, and I wished my mom could have seen me.

That day, at the top of the rope, I looked up over the rafters of the warehouse gym and felt a sense of accomplishment wash over me. As I looked down at my descent, I suddenly remembered how scared I am of heights. The adrenaline was fading, and I quickly slid down and planted myself on the cushy foam mat. "What next?" I thought to myself.

As my feet sank into the mat on the ground, I realized I wasn't satisfied with just meeting my goal. I wanted another physical challenge to silence the grief that was always brewing in the back of my mind. God gently spoke to me at that moment and reminded me: "You can't go back, Trina. No physical challenge or goal is going to make you who you were before she died." I had been toughing out my grief without asking for help or assistance from God. There was nothing anchoring me as I tried to pull myself up on my own strength. Thankfully, God is like a persistent and wise trainer. If you put a little bit of trust in him, he will transform your faith into something that can move mountains. He is overjoyed by our trust in him, no matter the outcome.

Dear Lord, I anchor my feet in your presence today.

I'm tired of trying to do this on my own.

No completed goal or accomplishment is going to bring back my loved one or make me feel better for long.

I need your guidance and strength. Amen.

DAY 62

HOPE FILLS YOU UP

Therefore encourage one another and build each other up, just as in fact you are doing. —1 Thessalonians 5:11 NIV

A light dusting of grief seemed to saturate the air like the sprinkle of cinnamon across the latte in front of me. The coffee shop was still, and the windows were fogged up from the hot steam of the espresso machine hitting the cold January air outside. I was meeting my friend Richelle for coffee to discuss having "moms with cancer," a club neither of us ever wanted to be members of. We never expected to be here. Nevertheless, here we were.

Just eight months earlier, Richelle and I had chatted on my wedding day as she pulled a hot curling iron through my hair and delicately painted eyeliner across my eyelids. I remember I looked up at her reflection in the mirror before me and felt grateful that she was chatting happily away and helping me forget just how strange it is to get married while your mom is dying. She had driven over three hours to do my hair and makeup for my wedding day. Most of my other bridesmaids were getting ready in the church bathroom, and the fireside room echoed with a quiet stillness with just the sound of brushes and my aunt's quiet chatter with my cousin. My mom held my hand while sitting beside me in her loaned wheelchair. Somehow, she had rallied that day, and it was no small miracle that she was there to witness this moment. Richelle's mom had not been diagnosed yet, and she got a front row seat to one of the most poignant and heartbreaking moments of my loss. I don't know if this was a kindness to prepare her for what was coming or a shocking orientation to the realities of loss. Perhaps it was a bit of both.

No matter what grief club we belong to, God pours his love into our hearts. He holds us as we hold their hands for those last big milestones. He knows that we must rely on each other in the hardest times. In the quiet hush of preparation, before the loud celebration of a wedding, he is there. Richelle almost didn't make it that day because of conflicting schedules, but she did. Her mom was still healthy, and my mom was not. There is something bonding about witnessing each other's pain. When I heard her mom was sick, I reached out to her, even though every part of me didn't want to open up my own pain. She had stood by me that rainy spring day and prepped my face to withstand all of the emotions. How could I run away from her tears now?

"My family is coming from all over, and we're snapping at each other. And there's so much ..." Richelle started to wave her arms around, searching for the right word to describe the chaos as we sipped lattes. "Drama? I volunteered. "There is so much family drama when cancer comes," I said, helping her finish the sentence. She sighed and nodded in agreement.

After that, I didn't feel quite so alone for a moment. Because, in her, I saw a reflection of my own hard and complicated pain.

We filled the quiet stillness of the coffee shop with laughter about the absurdity of grief. We never expected to be here, but I'm so glad we both showed up.

Dear God, I never expected to be here.

And yet, here I am.

Help me to not feel alone and to bear witness
to my experiences today.

We are meant to encourage one another
and build each other up.

Help me to show up for somebody else today. Amen.

DAY 63

REMEMBERING OUR LOVED ONES

But then I recall all you have done, O Lord; I remember your wonderful deeds of long ago. They are constantly in my thoughts. I cannot stop thinking about your mighty works.
—Psalm 77:11–12 NLT

My mom smiled at me from the kitchen. But it was only an image of her, framed in bright silver. My sister had gathered several of my mom's portraits, and my family all went home with one after the memorial service. In the photo, my mom is mid-laugh, her bright brown eyes looking up. It was taken on the day of my sister's wedding, and pink peonies from the bridal bouquet framed my mom's shoulders. She was glowing with happiness as the mother-of-the-bride. I tried putting her photo on my bedside table, but it didn't seem right. I tried the bookshelf too, since she loved to read. None of these places was the right fit for her picture. Finally, I placed her on top of the windowsill, right above the kitchen sink. "That feels right," I thought to myself because mom was in the kitchen once again. I thought it was just a picture of my mom, but it represented my memories of her too.

God wants to capture my attention when I look at my mom's portrait. He wants me to remember my mom's love as I go about my daily life. He does not turn away from my grief but feels compassion toward me. When Jesus met a widow grieving the loss of her son, the Bible says, "His heart went out to her and he said, 'Don't cry'" (Luke 7:13 NIV). He didn't ignore her but stopped what he was doing to meet her needs. He told her, "Don't cry," because he was about to bring her son back to life. I don't know why God didn't heal my mom too, but I do know that his love remains. His heart goes out to me as I grieve her death and remember who she was.

I think it's important to create spaces where we can allow ourselves to grieve. Maybe that means framing a picture of your loved one or writing them a letter. Maybe you could share memories of them with a friend. I know some people find it comforting to keep an old shirt of their person in their closet that they can pull out when they miss them. Everybody grieves differently, but memories are always important. God sees our pain and wants to meet us there in our moments of grief.

My grief likes to be set out on the windowsill, taking in the light. It's a constant observer of my everyday tasks, like washing the dishes, making coffee, and sweeping the floors. It watches over me in a gentle, but constant, way. For some, grief likes to be tucked away in a sock drawer, like a treasured love letter you can pull out from time to time to reread. Neither approach to grief is better than the other—both can be pictures of healthy processing.

Dear Jesus, help me to sort through my memories today—the good, the bad, and the ones I don't ever want to let go of.

Whether my grief looks like a treasured portrait on the windowsill or one safely kept in a drawer, you meet me where I am. Amen.

DAY 64

KNOWN AND LOVED

I tell you the truth, anyone who doesn't receive the Kingdom of God like a child will never enter it. —Mark 10:15 NLT

At the bottom of the Cheerios box we stored our Christmas ornaments in laid my favorite ornament as a child. It was a metal red-and-green train with the year "1987" on its side. As a six-year-old, I asked my dad what the meaning of this ornament was. I was curious about why my parents kept an ornament from 1987 when it wasn't their anniversary or the year of any of our births. He told me that mom had been pregnant with a baby who had died around Christmastime. I later learned that my mom had undergone two miscarriages before my sister was born two years later. A boy and a girl that we never got to meet. As a child, I thought of heaven as the place where I could someday meet my other siblings. I didn't think about it much, other than at Christmastime when the ornament came back out—when I remembered my dad's sweet gift to my mom to try to cheer her up.

When I was in high school, we had a youth leader Q&A session, and my mom was one of the leaders up front. One of the anonymous questions written on folded-up paper was: "Have you ever experienced depression?" My mom volunteered to take the mic. As a seventeen-year-old, I froze in my chair, surprised to see her reaching for the microphone: "Why is my mom talking about depression?" To a crowd of teenagers, she talked openly about how she felt depressed after losing her babies, and I sat in awe of her bravery. At that moment, I remembered the Christmas ornament and how I would put my mother's grief away, year after year, as if it were an ornament tucked in a cardboard box, hidden in the corner of the attic. I thought she had too, but in reality, she always carried it with her next to her beating heart.

How do we remain here on this earth when we are always grieving someone who died too soon? Nobody likes to talk about people dying young or miscarriages. Oftentimes, people don't know how to acknowledge or talk about this particular kind of grief. Yet for those of us living out this reality, we need to talk about it. Like a precious ornament on a tree, there needs to be space to display our love for the person we lost in order to remember them. There are no answers or resolutions to a life taken too soon. All I know is that, for my mom, those little babies were completely loved and known by her. And she wanted to tell their story.

But Jesus said, "Let the children come to me, and don't try to stop them! People who are like these children belong to God's kingdom" (Matthew 19:14 CEV). Jesus let the children come to him, talk to him, and be blessed by him. His followers tried to shoo them away because they seemed like a distraction from the more important things. Instead, Jesus showed them that *they* were the important thing. Jesus values and sees the people others overlook. If you feel alone or ignored because your grief feels invisible to others, know that Jesus embraces the overlooked and forgotten. Let Jesus take you into his arms, place his hands on your head, and bless you today because your grief is important to him.

Dear God, there are no barriers around you
when I seek you out.

I can approach you boldly and with confidence.

You do not forget me.

You always remember me and the ones I have lost.
Amen.

DAY 65

EAGERLY WAITING

So Christ, having been offered once to bear the sins of many, will appear a second time, not to deal with sin but to save those who are eagerly waiting for him. —Hebrews 9:28 ESV

As a highly imaginative child, I pictured God's love like the great sky above me. One summer day when I was four years old, I was running around our cul-de-sac when the clouds filled up with rain, and I felt like I was standing in the eye of the storm. The hot pavement released the tangy and cool scent of wet concrete. I thought to myself, "I feel like an astronaut! I'm flying all the way to heaven!" I started zooming around the sidewalk like a space explorer. I can't quite explain it, but as a kid, I could sense God's love in the air that day.

God's presence is a wondrous thing that should fill us with awe and an expectation of his return. His love is akin to a thunderstorm sometimes. The psalmist describes God in this way: "The clouds poured out water; the skies gave forth thunder; your arrows flashed on every side. The crash of your thunder was in the whirlwind; your lightnings lighted up the world; the earth trembled and shook" (Psalm 77:17–18 ESV). A few days after my mom died, I sat with my dad and sister on the front porch of my parents' house, watching a summer thunderstorm above us. The sky was completely gray with streaks of lightning. We counted the seconds together between the flashes of light and the rumblings of thunder in order to judge the distance. The rain hitting the pavement filled my nostrils with the same sharp scent that I noticed as a child. It felt to us like mom was pounding the skies, sending us one final message that she loved us and was OK. Our grief flashed like lightning, striking the skies, and God's love rumbled an echo, reminding us that he is always near.

God is coming back for us one day—not as a distant figure in the sky but as a friend calling us home. Jesus promised that he would come back to save those of us eagerly waiting for him. We are living for so much more than this life. We are destined for eternity and for the reconciliation of all things. I know that God is coming back because I have seen the lightning, and I'm waiting now for the thunder. Here I am, rooted in the here-and-now of this earth, but looking toward the heavens for his return. I know that the thundering of my grief will someday fade when I see him face to face. And I long for that day.

Dear Jesus, I sense your love in your creation—
the sky above and the earth below.

Things feel more complicated now,
as I wrestle with death in a fallen world.

You say that you will return one day to save
those who eagerly wait for you, and so here I am,
waiting for you. Amen.

DAY 66

FAITH SHARES ITS STORY WITH OTHERS

In the last days, God says, I will pour my Spirit on everyone.
Your sons and daughters will speak what God has revealed.
Your young men will see visions.
Your old men will dream dreams. —Acts 2:17 GW

I stared back at my reflection in the bathroom mirror, wiping my sweaty palms on the black fabric of my skirt, folding and unfolding the paper in the pocket of my jean jacket. And that's when the doubts started flooding in: "Are you really the person to do this? Did your friend really mean to ask you? Quick! Run out to the parking lot and drive home and tell them you got the stomach flu!" My friend Kristi had asked me to share a poem at our women's ministry Christmas tea. Minutes before the program started, I had rushed to the bathroom in a panic. The poem I had written was about Christmas presents—how grief was a package I never wanted to arrive, but one I was coming to terms with.

It was sad and poignant and something I was excited to share. Until that moment.

I remembered my mom sharing with me about how she would always get hit with a massive headache or some other seemingly random obstacle right before she would get up to preach at her women's Bible study. My mom loved public speaking, and as a high school Spanish teacher, she was comfortable talking in front of any group of people in two different languages. Yet when she stepped out to share with the ladies, she experienced spiritual warfare. It wasn't demons with swords or anything glaringly obvious like that, but I believe that when we step out to share our stories, we will often encounter obstacles and doubts like darts from the devil. Please don't let this stop you!

Someone needs to hear you share your story when you're ready and the moment is right. It doesn't have to be a formal speech; it could be during a walk or a game of pickup basketball. Or maybe you are asked to share in front of people or in a group. For all of us, there will come a time when we are asked to share our stories. The best part about sharing our stories is that it's not about *us*. It's about what God has done and is doing. It's about the one person who needs to hear it. If you make one person's burdens lighter for one day, isn't that worth the nerves and discomfort? You are already a thoughtful person who is taking the time to work through your grief, so don't get self-conscious about being attention-seeking or whatever doubts may be plaguing you. You do not have to share more than you're comfortable with, and know that you've probably already shared a lot of your story with others just by living honestly before them.

That cold December night, I stepped up to the microphone, cleared my throat, and said, "Three years ago, dreams of engagement boxes danced above my head ..." The faces in the audience faded as I looked to the exit signs in the back and sent up a quick prayer for courage. I finished the poem, and my tablemate squeezed my arm as I sat back down at my seat. She said, "That was beautiful. Thank you." I smiled and thought to myself, "Mom would be proud of me."

Dear God, reveal to me the opportunities
you have placed before me to begin to share
my story with others.

Protect me from the enemy's attacks
and don't let it stop me from doing good.

Show me where I need to step into the light
and be brave. Amen.

DAY 67

HOPE IN THE THINGS TO COME

The Lord *your God is with you; his power gives you victory. The* Lord *will take delight in you, and in his love he will give you new life. He will sing and be joyful over you.*
—Zephaniah 3:17 GNT

When my mom's health started to decline, my dad transferred all the VHS tapes of our home videos into a digital format so we could all have copies of them. We went back and watched different memories together in the days following my mom's death. One of those moments was Christmas Eve in 1996, when my dad dressed up as Santa, and all of us kids danced with him in the living room as the boombox radio blasted "Joy to the World." We all knew dad wasn't *really* Santa, and it was commonplace to dance around the living room together. But watching that tape, as I grieved my mom's death, I couldn't help but glimpse the divinity of God in the familiarity of a family memory.

It was sacred because it represented God's fatherly love toward us. My dad twirled each of us girls across the carpet, and my two-year-old brother wandered aimlessly in circles. The angelic voices of a choir permeated the room from the boombox perched on top of the TV stand. My mom laughed, unseen behind the giant camcorder. The clip soon cut out after that because we all started having meltdowns as our bedtime approached. We started laughing hysterically as we tried to bounce off Santa's fake belly and bonked heads with each other. The magic of the moment was over, but it stuck with me.

Watching that clip felt like she was still there, watching me twirling and dancing through life, trying to make sense of it all without her. Oftentimes, it feels like I am in the process of a meltdown—dizzy and overwhelmed with grief. But I feel her right there with me, just like when she was behind the camcorder that day, laughing and smiling, always ready to scoop me up and tuck me into bed. It isn't the same, of course, and that feeling of her closeness melts like a tender snowflake falling as soon as I try to grasp it.

The morning after our Christmas Eve Santa dance, we woke up to drifts of snow that reached above my waist. My parents pulled up the blinds behind our Christmas tree and surprised us with a wooden playhouse in the back of my dad's pickup truck. It looked magical with a dusting of snow coating the blue roof. It was transcendent, and I will remember it far beyond the clips captured in that home video.

I don't know what heaven is like, and any guesses I have wouldn't come close to the reality. But I do know that heaven will include the goodness of relationships and that we will experience a closeness we never achieved on earth. We might even find ourselves dancing with the Father as people from all nations declare, "Joy to the World." I pray today that you find the barriers and distance between you and God removed. That you will no longer be merely an observer of his presence but an active participant in it.

Dear God, you dance over me with joy and singing.

You delight in me, and your love gives me new life (Zephaniah 3:17).

I look forward to the day when we can be even closer in heaven.

For now, open my eyes to the relationships in front of me that reveal your divine nature. Amen.

DAY 68

LOVE WELCOMES THE GRIEVER IN

The bodies we now have are weak and can die. But they will be changed into bodies that are eternal. Then the Scriptures will come true, "Death has lost the battle! Where is its victory? Where is its sting?" —1 Corinthians 15:54–55 CEV

The first Easter after my mom died, I stepped up large concrete steps toward a navy, two-story home, ready to knock on the front door. Every Easter, my friend Alex and her husband Justin would throw a party they affectionately called "orphan Easter," which was for anyone who needed a place to go during the holiday, and they had invited me because my husband was working Easter day. This tradition began as a way to love people who couldn't go home and see family for Easter, and eventually, it evolved into an open invitation to anyone at their church, work, or the neighborhood they lived in.

That day, I stood on their doorstep waiting to go inside. I remember the sounds of a child's tricycle bell and the smell of the damp daffodils lining the path on that rainy spring afternoon. I held a goat cheese platter, and the plastic wrap clung to my hands. "Is it too late to turn around, go home, and change into sweats and watch my favorite shows until my husband gets off work?" I asked myself. But before I could change my mind and run back to my car, Alex swung the front door wide open, grinned down at me, and said, "Hello, Katrina! Come on in!" She whisked me inside and quickly traded my plate for a mimosa. Folding tables stretched across their living room where adults chatted and children ran around with happy giggles. I sat at the table with a full plate of roasted asparagus and salted ham and met a family who had recently relocated from the Midwest. I watched Alex's dad chase his grandkids up the stairs. Their home was bursting with life.

The idea of "orphan Easter" resonated with me because I did not have my mom anymore. I felt like an outsider because the celebration of God conquering death felt like early morning light on tired eyes. I said to myself, "I believe Jesus has risen and defeated death, so why does death still sting? How do I celebrate love conquering death?"

Maybe you've asked yourself these same questions at some point, and you are not the only one to be asking them. After Mary found Jesus's empty tomb, she wept. She was so blinded by grief that she did not know her Savior stood beside her. "He asked her, 'Woman, why are you crying? Who is it you are looking for?' Thinking he was the gardener, she said, 'Sir, if you have carried him away, tell me where you have put him, and I will get him.' Jesus said to her, 'Mary.' She turned toward him and cried out in Aramaic, 'Rabboni!' (which means 'Teacher')" (John 20:15–16

NIV). When Jesus called her name, she knew him. She knew he had conquered death. Jesus rising from the dead is good news because it means he invites us personally in and calls us by name. "Why are you crying? I'm here!" he tells us.

A few years later, my friend Alex sat next to my sister at church. Alex had recently lost her dad to cancer—the man who had been chasing his grandkids at "orphan Easter." He had a larger-than-life presence, and Alex had inherited his same generosity of spirit. She turned to my sister and told her, "Looking at you, and seeing that you're still going, even after your mom died, gives me hope that someday I'll be able to function too." Sometimes it's our turn to open our doors wide and welcome people in when they feel discouraged and overwhelmed by grief. Other times, it's our turn to take shelter in the presence of those who love us and call us by name. When we recognize grief in each other's eyes and turn toward each other in recognition of God's hope, we celebrate Christ's resurrection all over again. Oh death, where is your sting?

Dear Jesus, be with me today as I wrestle with feelings of grief and abandonment.

It's not easy to acknowledge my grief or open myself up to other people.

You always invite me in and call me by name.

You rose from the dead and that is something I can celebrate, even as I grieve.

Help me today to recognize your hope in the generosity of others. Amen.

DAY 69

TIME TO CRY, TIME TO LAUGH

There is a time for everything, and a season for every activity under the heavens. —Ecclesiastes 3:1 NIV

I just couldn't stop making cinnamon rolls," she said to me, leaning over her cup of coffee. My friend Kathleen was telling me about her first Christmas after her mom died. "I pulled pan after pan of cinnamon rolls out of the hot oven, and no one could stop me." I nodded and laughed, remembering the first Christmas without my mom, and how I found myself in a similar predicament. My sister and I had ambitiously decided to replicate the baking my mom had done. It was as if I thought the oven could bake away the grief and the comfort of familiar foods could fill the gaping hole of her absence. Instead, that Christmas I was left jittery from drinking too much coffee and flushed from too much time near the hot oven. Hearing a similar story from a friend made me realize that the holidays are ripe with strong emotions because of all the unmet expectations. I knew I couldn't replicate the past or replace my mom, but something in me had to try to make the same foods she did anyway. Instead of bringing me comfort, it left me anxious and confused.

Feeling on the verge of a panic attack that day, I escaped to the coolness of the garage and sat beside the marinating turkey in a stockpot, where I let myself cry. The hustle of the kitchen could only temporarily abate the waters of grief. "Jesus, this is hard," I prayed. I wish I could go back and tell myself that I wasn't alone—that there were other people struggling during the holidays too. I wish I could have told myself that those first holidays are like raw dough, unformed and untested in the oven of grief. I would tell myself that it doesn't get easier. Instead, I would develop bigger muscles to wrestle the dough. Or maybe, I would just sit next to my past self until we started to laugh about how funny it was to cry next to raw poultry.

I can view the loneliest, hardest holidays with compassion now because God has shown me that there's an appropriate time for every emotion. Some people find comfort in throwing themselves into projects, but I have to set aside time first to just sit and cry during the holidays. I'm learning that there's a time to cry, a time to laugh, and a time to marathon bake cinnamon rolls.

Dear Jesus, I really need to talk to you today.

This hurts. This is really hard.

I'm trying to recreate some of the holiday spirit I had before, and it's not working out like I thought it would.

You remind me that there is a time for every emotion.

Help me to create space to cry so that, when I'm ready to laugh and celebrate, I can. Amen.

DAY 70

REMAIN HERE, WHEN THEY'RE NOT

And we know that for those who love God all things work together for good, for those who are called according to his purpose.
—Romans 8:28 ESV

Two years after my mom died, I went to a women's breakfast in my church's multipurpose room. The walls were decorated with giant, handmade paper flowers, and there were antique plates on each table. It used to be the main sanctuary until the late '90s, and it was where my parents had exchanged vows in 1984. In their wedding photos, my mom had dark permed curls, and my dad had a wispy mustache which gave him a youthful look. As I stood in that same room, I felt close to the memory of her and that special day. But my reverie into the past was soon interrupted by the anxious thought: "You still haven't found a place to live!"

Our current place was being converted into a vacation rental, and we only had a month until we needed to move out. A week before then, everything seemed to be lined up for us to move into a cozy rental with lake views until someone outbid us for the rent price. I had already started dreaming about typing away at the kitchen table with a serene lake to offer me inspiration. I was annoyed at God for seeming like he "offered" this dream only to snatch it away.

My introspective thoughts were again interrupted when my friend Alex kneeled next to me at my table and said, "Hey! I heard you guys need a place to live. We just bought a house on the lake, and it has a rental. Are you interested?" "Yes, I'm very interested," I told her. My dream of living the lake life had been dangled before me, snatched away, and out of the blue, a new and even better opportunity came about. Life doesn't always work out this way, but when it does, I have to laugh. I like to raise my hands up to the sky and say, "You're up to something God!" because sometimes he works in the most mysterious and merciful ways.

As the good news of a place to live sunk in, I thought to myself, "How do I remain here where my mom is not?" Even the good and abundant things seemed to come with the price of her absence. I kept picking up my phone to try to call her. Once again, I couldn't. As my grandma liked to tell me: "Heaven is a little more long-distance than my phone can handle." It felt strange to be looking at a new place without her. She had never even seen our first rental, but I had talked to her about it and shown her pictures. I wanted so badly to tell her about our new lake house and to hear her inevitable jokes about me living a cushy lake life of ease and tranquility. She was my first place of safety and refuge, but she wasn't my only source of safety and refuge. I needed to find peace in the security that Jesus offers us as his children. No matter what happens, he is for us; he is always working things together for our good. It is our job to trust in him as we live between this life and the life to come—to be here when our loved ones are not.

Dear God, if I remain in you and in your love,
I know that you will work all things out for good.

I wish I could share all the exciting things happening
in my life with my person, and it's hard to move
forward without them.

Thank you for good and unexpected gifts.

Your ways are merciful and mysterious,
and I stand in awe of you. Amen.

DAY 71

FAITH LAYERS ON THE HEALING

Cast your cares on the Lord *and he will sustain you; he will never let the righteous be shaken.* —Psalm 55:22 NIV

I balanced a large tower of Styrofoam layers, which was a visual representation of a wedding cake, toward an engaged couple sitting underneath the front shop window. The foam layers could be stacked in different arrangements to give couples an idea of the height and depth of their future cake. The couple before me had no idea this was my first wedding cake consultation. A flutter went through my stomach as I started my spiel about serving sizes and buttercream finishes. I had completed hundreds of cake orders before, but a wedding cake is a big deal; it will remain in pictures forever. Some people freeze a slice and eat it a year later. Your customers will either give glowing reviews, or you will be the consultant who didn't advise them to order enough cake for all their guests. High stakes, high pressure.

The next thirty minutes passed in a flurry of servings sizes, buttercream textures, and filling choices. They settled on a three-tier cake covered in soft waves of buttercream mimicking the ocean. One layer would be chocolate salted caramel; the middle was lemon with raspberry filling; and the third would be classic vanilla. I filled out the paper form with shaky hands as they left the shop beaming and chattering happily about their favorite flavors.

After I filed away the wedding order and stood on my tippy-toes to place the foam layers on top of the cake order fridge, I did a happy dance that everything had gone so smoothly, and I was excited for the next consultation. At that moment, I realized I was finally in a stable place with my grief. It had not diminished. It had not lessened. I had simply learned that some of the time I could balance my grief like layers of an elaborate cake so that I could help other people with their grief. I know now how to talk about it and be comfortable with pauses or not having the exact right words—how to guide my story into a sweet gift presented to others, even if my hands shake a little.

Unlike a wedding cake consultation, my grief no longer had a deadline or extra pressure of high expectations. By conquering my fears and trying something new, I gained confidence in my grief too. I realized that God's love for me wasn't dependent upon how well I was "coping" with my grief. Grief would always be carried in my heart, but that didn't mean I wouldn't move forward. My mom would have loved that I was helping people order wedding cakes, but I wasn't doing it just to make her happy. I was beginning to plan, dream, and gain confidence in my abilities without her support. Even as I juggled the what-ifs of grief, God gently guided me to heal slowly until I could begin to see my own personal transformation.

Moving forward with your life is not the same thing as leaving behind the person you loved. Be patient with yourself as you grow in new areas. Be patient with yourself as your life begins to look different. Be patient with yourself as you find your way. And when you feel lost, cast your cares on the Lord, for he will not let you be shaken.

Dear God, you do not judge my grieving nor do you ask me to carry the burden alone.

When I offer it up to you, you offer your kindness, acceptance, and faithfulness to ease the heaviness of grief.

You take my shaking hands and hold them.

You take my fluttering heart and say, "Peace, be still."

I love you. Amen.

DAY 72

HOPE DESTROYS FEAR

In my alarm I said, "I am cut off from your sight!" Yet you heard my cry for mercy when I called to you for help.
—Psalm 31:22 NIV

I soaked up every changing season the year we lived on Lake Samish. I admired the snow-tinged mountains lined with the sunset's rays. I basked in October's explosion of color on the hills as I sat on the dock. August's lingering heat baked my shoulders as I arced my feet in a gentle dive, transitioning to smooth strokes across the water. Spring meant long walks admiring wet grasses bordering the lake and soft petals falling into its blue embrace. When I moved in, I thought to myself, "The worst part of grief is probably over."

And yet, I cried. And yet, I grieved. And yet, food still didn't taste right on my tongue, and I was a little bit more depressed than I wanted to admit to myself or anyone else. "I live on a lake! How could I still be experiencing these periods of intense sadness?" I wondered to myself. It turns out that changing my view outside did little to change what was happening inside of me at the time. Nature doesn't cure all, and beauty doesn't solve everything. We can be living life fully, deeply, and intensely, and still, grief's heaviest burdens linger.

Something had to change in me to make things lighter—not externally but internally. One time when I was swimming in the lake, I turned around to see my friend's kids cheering me on from their porch. I waved back at them, smiling to myself. To their young minds, swimming across the lake was a huge achievement. Sometimes grieving is like that: you're pushing and pulling against the dark waters, slowly making progress and feeling tired, as if you aren't going anywhere. And unbeknownst to you, there are tiny cheerleaders jumping up and down, thinking you're amazing because you can swim that far.

God watches us with the same jubilant celebration and anticipation as we navigate these waters of grief. He knows if you're a little bit more depressed, anxious, or angry than you would like to admit. He knows you're overwhelmed by the beauty and that you really want to be able to experience it again: to taste the flaky sea salt on chocolate chip cookies and break the uppermost layer of water tension as you glide across it. Instead of only contemplating, "Is the worst of my grief over yet?" God invites us to celebrate how far we have already come.

God wanted me to continue to heal, not just on the outside but deep within my heart. And the first step was admitting how I was feeling. With raw honesty and depth of conviction, I had to say it out loud. I'm anxious. I'm depressed. I'm sad. I talked to God about it and to people close to me whom I trusted. It was time to dive into the dark waters of my fear in order to emerge from the surface, ready to face the truth.

Dear Jesus, it's so hard to be honest today.

Yes, I'm struggling.

Yes, this life, even with its most beautiful views, cannot fix my grief.

Even when I have felt cut off from you, I know "you heard my cry for mercy when I called to you for help" (Psalm 31:22 NIV).
Amen.

DAY 73

LOVE'S OPEN INVITATION

But me! I will keep watch for the L*ORD; I will wait for the God of my salvation; my God will hear me.* —Micah 7:7 CEB

The day of my mom's memorial service, I kept thinking I saw her around each corner of the church building. It wasn't eerie like a ghost; my brain just didn't know how to continue without her presence, so it was trying to piece together the strangeness of her absence. "We've left her behind. We've forgotten her," I kept thinking. I've since learned that this is a common phenomenon of grieving people. My grieving brain was not always rational, but there was often a pattern to its irrationality. My brain wanted to make sense of the senseless, and so I had to use my four senses to pull it back into the present.

I tried deep breathing, finding four items of the same color around me, or listing out something I could smell, see, and hear. Sometimes I would place a small rock in my pocket that I could grab when I needed it. Maybe these ideas will help you too. Grasping the tangible can help us survive the intangible losses that rest heavily on our shoulders. Every little thought can bring us back to a memory or a connection to our loved ones. Thoughts like: "Remember when?" "I had hoped for ..." "We could've ..." "I should tell them ..." Like a forgotten glove left on the ground behind us, our thoughts can feel mismatched to the reality we are living in. It can feel lonely sometimes.

I loved my mom so much, and I *still* love her. Some days it still hits me, like a punch in the gut, that I can't hug her anymore. I would do anything to say hello and tell her about my life. On those days, I talk to her anyway. I write her a letter with a real pen and paper and tell her everything that's happening in my life. I go for a walk outside and put headphones in so people think I'm chatting on the phone, but really, I'm talking to her. When I see her favorite bird, drink, or color, I raise a proverbial glass in return and say, "Hello, Mom." I don't catch myself thinking she's right around the corner anymore, but sometimes, I still see her in my dreams. The pain is still guttural, instinctual, habitual, and *there*.

I have not forgotten her, nor have I left her behind. When you love someone, it just isn't possible to forget them. My mom's presence and memory follow me everywhere. One night, I had a dream that she gave me a big hug, and I woke up longing for it to be true. Later that morning at church, I was filling up my mug with coffee when one of the greeters came up to me and handed me a program. "Would you like a hug?" she asked me. I didn't know her, but somehow, she knew my need. It reminded me that God has not left me behind, and he doesn't forget about me. "Sure," I said, and she pulled me into a hug. "Hello, Mom," I thought in my head, as the lady walked away, unaware of the impact she had made.

Dear God, I am undone today.

My brain is weary of trying to make sense of my grief.

I can't forget my loved one, and I don't want to.

I know that you will hear me and respond to my pain (Micah 7:7).

Ground me in your presence today
through tangible things like walks outside,
beautiful colors, and the kindness of strangers.
Amen.

DAY 74

REMAIN PRESENT DURING GRIEF

Let everything that has breath and every breath of life praise the L*ORD! Praise the* L*ORD! (Hallelujah!)* —Psalm 150:6 AMP

Grief can be a persistent presence, constantly nagging you for your attention. You might be riding the bus and burst into tears with little provocation. Maybe you are walking the aisles of the grocery store and forget why you needed to go there in the first place. Your roommate starts telling you about their day, and you can't focus at all. A driver might cut you off in traffic, and you scream in frustration, whereas before, you would have merely waved it off. What is happening?

Grief affects everyone differently, but it doesn't leave anyone unaffected. Maybe you cope with it by over-performing. You've poured yourself into work, or relationships, or achievements and can barely stop to breathe because you are scared of what will happen if you pause. Or you draw inward, and no one knows where you are or how to help you. How do we remain present in our lives when grief feels so disruptive?

One way I like to remain present with my grief is to focus on my breath. I'm not trying to fight or fix my grief, but rather, give it space. God created our bodies to function best when we are getting the air we need, so why not take some time to just breathe? I like to try breath prayers to ground myself and make space for my grief. Breath prayers break down a piece of Scripture into two parts: one you recite as you breathe in and another you say as you breathe out. Here are some examples I like to use:

> *Inhale*: The Spirit of God has made me
> *Exhale*: and the breath of the Almighty gives me life.
> (Job 33:4 ESV)

> *Inhale*: The Lord *is* my shepherd;
> *Exhale*: I shall not want. (Psalm 23:1 KJV)

Try one out and see if it works for you. It might feel awkward or uncomfortable at first, but with practice, it really and truly does help you stay grounded and present. Breathing deeply has been found to have a myriad of health benefits, including an improved immune system and brain, heart, and digestive functions. You can't control when grief pops up, but you can return to your breath. Simply inhale. Exhale. Inhale. And exhale again.

Dear God, you gave me the breath of life
when you created me.

When I take the time to recognize this gift,
I find myself growing quieter inside.

I want so badly to control my grief, and sometimes
I have to let that go.

I praise you with my breath today, and I ask for peace.
Amen.

DAY 75

REMAIN AWARE OF YOUR BODY

During the days of Jesus' life on earth, he offered up prayers and petitions with fervent cries and tears to the one who could save him from death, and he was heard because of his reverent submission. —Hebrews 5:7–9 NIV

I lay curled up on the loveseat sofa, an ice pack cradling my forehead, with all the blinds drawn. It was the second-year anniversary of my mom's death, and I was hit with the pulsing ache of a migraine attack. My body knew the date on the calendar before my mind. Suddenly, a small child's face was inches away from mine with a wide grin. "We baked cookies! Do you want one?" My landlord's six-year-old son had come down the stairs to our rental to let me know they were making cookies. I had to laugh to myself at the contrast between his joy and my migraine attack. That's life sometimes. Our bodies hold and react to our grief, yet joy still fights to break through the shades of sadness.

My body often reacts to grief anniversaries with headaches that can turn into migraines. The only thing I can do once a migraine hits is to lie in the dark with an ice pack and listen to comedy podcasts. My doctor told me that if you miss the window for migraine medicine, the only thing to do is ride the wave of pain. Grief can sometimes feel similar, like a wave you have to ride out until it breaks on the shore.

Although I hate migraines, it makes me feel validated to know that the grief I carry is very real and it affects every part of me, even my physical body. It's as though some part of me *knows* that it misses her and remembers the loss before I cognitively recognize it in my brain. Grief is powerful stuff and knocks you down until you take the time to tend to it. It's why we must be attentive to our grief and give it the space and time it needs.

Jesus is no stranger to excruciating pain. The night before he was going to be arrested and later executed, he was talking to God in a garden. He was in such agony that he sweated blood from his forehead. His grief over what was to come transferred from his spiritual side into the physical realm. Jesus was facing a trifecta of hurt: 1) a public and shameful death; 2) torture and excruciating pain; and 3) worst of all, temporary but complete separation and abandonment from God.

Those days when I'm lying in a dark, quiet room and tempted to beat myself up for not accomplishing anything, I remember a God who sweated blood in the early hours of morning beneath a grove of olive trees. I know I'm not alone and that the same Jesus who suffered in that garden is with me. And one day, the joy is going to break through.

Dear Jesus, you bled and died for me on the cross,
but sometimes I forget about that quiet night
of torment in the garden before your public shame.

You've experienced excruciating pain on this earth
and understand my own pain.

You give me care and attention on my grief days.

Help me to see the joy too, not just the pain. Amen.

DAY 76

FAITH WAITS FOR THE LORD

Before the Passover celebration, Jesus knew that his hour had come to leave this world and return to his Father. He had loved his disciples during his ministry on earth, and now he loved them to the very end. —John 13:1 NLT

Several weeks before my mom died, I waited for the train to take me back up north to my home in Bellingham, Washington. I sat in the grass outside of the train station across from turf farms and suburban neighborhoods with my dad beside me. It would have been a lovely spring afternoon, if not for the heavy truth weighing on our minds like a freight car: my mom was dying. The next time I would return, it would be to say my final goodbye. I was already grieving her death preemptively, as I faced the inevitable conclusion of her disease. I was desperate for God to make sense of the loss I could see coming.

That day I experienced anticipatory grief, which is when you grieve a loss before it happens.[5] Grieving didn't start the day my mom died; it began as soon as the diagnosis hit. Jesus relates to and understands my anticipatory grief because he himself walked into Jerusalem already knowing he would be arrested, tortured, and killed in that city. Shortly before his death, Jesus told his disciples, "You will be scattered. … You will leave me alone. Yet I am not alone, for my Father is with me" (John 16:32 NIV). His execution and betrayal were imminent, and yet he desired peace for his friends. He told them these things so that instead of being discouraged they could "take heart"; for he has "overcome the world" (John 16:33 NIV). As Jesus grieved the losses coming, he also offered them hope.

As the train came to a hissing stop, and the ticket master helped me carry my luggage up the steps, I thought, "Where are you Jesus? What's going to happen next?" As I settled into my seat, I waved at my dad, standing next to the train, through the window. I held back my tears until he was out of sight. As I grieved the next part of my life going in a direction I didn't choose, Jesus was preparing my heart for what came next. Great sorrow was coming next, but that didn't mean joy was gone forever too.

---

5. *Anticipatory Grief: Preparing for a Loved One's End of Life,* https://www.cancercare.org/publications/385-anticipatory_grief_preparing_for_a_loved_one_s_end_of_life.

Dear Jesus, as I wait for the trains of life to take me to places I want to go, and the places I never want to go, you are along for the ride.

"Wait for the LORD; be strong and take heart and wait for the LORD" (Psalm 27:14 NIV).

Help me to be strong as I wait for you to make yourself apparent.

No matter the type of grief I feel, you are with me. Amen.

DAY 77

HOPE IN THE PROMISES OF GOD

I remain confident of this: I will see the goodness of the L*ORD* *in the land of the living.* —Psalm 27:13 NIV

As I laid down in the wet grass beside a lemon tree, I contemplated how I had bought lemons but never seen one on a tree. Growing up in Washington state, I had only ever seen apple or pear trees grow. But the mild, sixty-degree weather of central California provides the perfect microclimate for citrus to flourish. My friend Rachel sat on the front porch of the house we were staying at with her knees pulled close to her, a knit cap pulled over her red hair, her tall frame shadowed by the porch lights. We were on a spring break trip to Davis, California, and several months earlier, Rachel's poem had been chosen to be read in front of our large Christian group. She shared about her mother's recent death and starry constellations, and I swear even the buzzing of the multipurpose room lights paused for a moment while she read. She talked of heaven and the vastness of space. She knew I liked to write poetry too, and we were both excited to be on the same trip. But now, Rachel was having a hard time.

"I just want to go home," Rachel said, holding her head in her hands. She turned to look at me, flopping like a starfish, pretending to do snow angels in the grass. I remembered her poem and said, "Wow! Look at the stars tonight. What a wonderful moment!" She laughed at me and shook her head because I was being more than a little ridiculous, trying to pull a smile from her. I didn't tell her then, but the Lord had warned me that morning that hard times were coming for me. I merely rested near the lemon tree that night, but Rachel had already tasted its fruit. My time was coming, but for one night, we were just two girls laughing under the stars.

At the end of the week, Rachel thanked me for cheering her up that night. She said she was feeling discouraged and my goofiness was just what she needed. I ran into Rachel at the dessert shop three years after our trip. She came in with her fiancé, and we caught up as I cut them slices of cake. After my mom died, I felt like all the humor and playfulness that was part of my personality disappeared overnight. Rachel's presence had a lightness and a hope to it, and it reminded me of the woman I used to be. It reminded me that I could find her again—the one who laughed easily and delighted in the world around her. Just because I was discouraged in my grief, didn't mean that hope was out of reach.

Even though I had tasted the bitter fruit of loss, Rachel reminded me that good things could still happen. God will be faithful to us during our sorrow, even on the days we can't see it. There's no need to try to make "lemonade out of lemons," when our true desire is for the presence of hope. If you're struggling today, remember this: we can be confident in God's goodness.

Dear Jesus, I remain confident that I will see
your goodness here on earth.

Your hope is real and available to me.

Thank you for the people who remind me that hope
and joy can always return to us.

Open my eyes to the stars tonight and how they reveal
your enduring promises to me.

Hold my head in your hands
and remind me to still hope. Amen.

DAY 78

LOVE IS A WORN NOTECARD IN YOUR POCKET

Encourage each other with psalms, hymns, and spiritual songs. Sing and make music in your hearts to the Lord. Always give thanks to God the Father for everything in the name of our Lord Jesus Christ. —Ephesians 5:19–20 ERV

The morning of February 20th, 2015, started like any other day. My alarm went off. I pulled on a sweater and made a cup of coffee. I shuffled my way down an icy hill to my car and drove into work. At work, I said hello to students I passed in the hall and settled into my desk tucked into the corner of the Care Room. Volunteers from the local university showed up, and I greeted them with a warm hello.

It felt like a perfectly ordinary day. One of the volunteers helping me was another Christian whom I knew from college. "Thanks for today," I told her as she grabbed her backpack to return to campus. She paused at my desk before heading out the door and said, "I feel like I'm supposed to give this to you." She handed me a small notecard with a Bible verse written on it: "My flesh and my heart may fail, but God is the strength of my heart and my portion forever" (Psalm 73:26 NIV).

"This is my grandma's favorite verse," she said, as I put it in the pocket of my jeans. "Thanks!" I told her, smiling. I thought it was a kind gesture and a testament to my friend's gentle awareness of how others were doing. She had no way of knowing that my mom had gone into the ER earlier because of a horrible headache because I had not told anyone at work. My brain had been dripping with worries like the icicles melting outside my window, and I hoped everything would be resolved quickly. There was no snowstorm of diagnosis yet.

The storm came later that day, after I got home from work. My dad called to say that they had results from the brain scans the ER doctor had ordered. My mom had multiple tumors in her brain. I crumpled into an angry ball on my bed, tears pouring from my eyes as I vacillated between shock and grief. I could see my bridal veil poking out of the wedding shop bag and that only made the questions roll over me like snowdrifts, burying my pain under the grim possibilities: "Was she going to die? Would she make it to my wedding? Would she survive to meet my future kids?" I began to punch the pillows of my bed with each question that fired through my brain. My anger quickly faded to numbness, and I called Jesse and told him between sobs what news I had just received. He promised to pick up Thai food and come over as soon as possible. I rolled over in my bed, no tears or punches left, just a heavy weariness. I put my hands in my pockets and felt the sharp edge of the notecard prick my finger.

God is the strength of my heart forever.

For a brief moment, those words melted away the flurries of shock so I could breathe. I carried that notecard in my pocket for the next four months while my mom was sick and for months after she died. Soon it was worn and soft with use. It sits now beside my wedding veil in a memento box, reminding me of a time when it grounded me to God's everlasting love, when every step I took felt unsteady.

God's eternal love was placed in my balled-up fists that day. My friend's thoughtfulness echoed out further than she probably realized. Maybe you need to write down a verse today too. It could be 1 Corinthians 13:13: "And now these three remain: faith, hope, and love but the greatest of these is love" (NIV) or Psalm 73:26. Maybe you could slip it into your pocket for later. Or maybe you should give it to someone else because we never know what God is up to. He takes our seemingly ordinary days and small acts of faithfulness and shows us extraordinary love.

Dear God, I come before you with many questions.

My hands shake with anger, and I do not understand
why things have to be this way.

My flesh and my heart fail, but you are my strength
forever (Psalm 73:26 NIV).

I ask for your truth to wash over me today
and become a comfort to my soul. Amen.

DAY 79

REMAIN FAITHFUL AMID THE DOUBTS

I have swept away your offenses like a cloud, your sins like the morning mist. Return to me, for I have redeemed you.
—Isaiah 44:22 NIV

I have found the calm presence of Jesus at train platforms, beside lemon trees, and in hospital rooms where I clutched Bible verses in my pockets. He has not been a casual observer of my loss but rather an active participant with me. As a young child, my favorite question was "Why?" I would ask my mom "Why?" over and over and over again as she drove the car. I still ask questions all the time, especially of God. My questions don't always get answers, but I've found comfort in Jesus's scarred hands, marked with angry red lines where men pounded nails into them. I can trace my doubts across his scars and feel the veins of truth.

After Jesus died and conquered death three days later, he appeared to his disciples. One of the first things he did was show them his scars, including to his friend Thomas. Thomas had questions for Jesus and doubted if it was *really* him. I've wondered to myself, "Why did Jesus still have scars? Why not present an unblemished version of himself? Why leave any trace of what had happened before?" Maybe because, without those scars, Thomas could not have touched them. Thomas couldn't have placed his fingers in the gnarled grooves of violence and confronted the reality of a risen Jesus before him.

Perhaps you want a perfect, unblemished version of yourself right now. You want to hide all your scars—the visible and invisible ones. As you begin to see the first traces of healing in your own life, you want to run away, as far as possible, from the pain that caused it in the first place. How do we remain steadfast in our healing process while integrating the wounded parts of ourselves?

A scarred Savior is not scared of my wounds. He does not shy away from the parts of my story that others cannot handle. He offers his own two hands before me and says, "See my pain. See the wounds made by this dark world. And yet, here I am. Here I stand, offering my scars to heal you." I don't have to hide the wounded parts of myself from him. He responds to my doubts by letting me trace the scars of his sacrifice.

Dear God, you did not hide your scars, so why should I hide mine from you?

I offer up all of my wounds before you today.

I can't help but ask "why?" and I love that you don't shrink away from my doubts.

You were marked so that I could find healing.

You offered yourself up as a sacrifice, even though you were perfect in every way.

I return to you because you have redeemed me. Amen.

DAY 80

REMAIN IN ME, AND I WILL REMAIN IN YOU

Remain in me, and I will remain in you. For a branch cannot produce fruit if it is severed from the vine, and you cannot be fruitful unless you remain in me. —John 15:4 NLT

The rickety ladder creaked beneath me as I reached up to grab ripe pears from the top of my grandma's tree. The late August heat was beating down, and I was bored after hours of picking berries. "Why are my mom and grandma so excited about fruit?" I thought to myself as I jumped down the rungs of the ladder. What had begun as a routine visit to grandma's house had turned into a berry-and-fruit-picking marathon with my mom and siblings. My empty stomach rumbled as I asked my mom: "Are we done yet?" Thankfully, my grandma opened the screen door and called us in for cold lemonade and chewy oatmeal cookies. Entering the house, we could smell the beginnings of dinner cooking on the stove, which was fresh garden peas cooked in heavy cream alongside salty slices of ham. We dumped our buckets of jewel-colored berries into large bowls and rinsed them in the sink. A day of hard work was *finally* done. Our car smelled of dust and the sharp tang of fresh fruit as we drove home and the sun set—our bellies and hearts full after a long day's work.

On the first anniversary of my mom's death, I struggled to figure out how to spend the day. My sister came up with the idea to go strawberry picking together. We found ourselves bent over rows of bright green strawberry plants, carefully selecting the ripest berries. I was grateful to not be alone that day, with my sister beside me, wearing my mom's straw hat. We didn't have to say much as we quietly worked side by side. The familiar sound of berries plunking into our pails brought me back to the days spent picking fruit beside my mom at grandma's house. I began to daydream about making homemade jam, pie, crumble, or just berries in a bowl with some whipped cream. I finally began to understand why my mom and grandma liked picking fruit. It wasn't just about the satisfaction of completing a task; it was about spending time together and enjoying the bounty of your harvest later on.

Grief sometimes feels like a long day under the unrelenting sun, with little fruit to show for it. When we endure hard things and question the point of continuing on, God says, "Remain in me and I will remain in you" (John 15:4 NLT). When we are tempted to rely on our own strength, God calls us to join him. He wants us close to him, like a branch grafted into a healthy vine. By his strength, our lives will produce good fruits. God also says, "I have loved you even as the Father has loved me. Remain in my love" (John 15:9 NLT). We can remain in his love because his love for us has been steadfast. When we labor with God, we will also share in the bountiful harvest when it comes.

Dear Lord, you remain in me as I remain in you.

As I abide in your presence, I ask that you would help
me work alongside you, not apart from you.

I want to share the grief-load with you,
so we can celebrate the bounty of joy
together as well. Amen.

DAY 81

FAITH IS A FIRM FOUNDATION

For no one can lay any foundation other than the one already laid, which is Jesus Christ. —1 Corinthians 3:11 NIV

When I was eighteen years old, the spiritual landscape of my soul exploded like fireworks on a dark Fourth of July night. Everything was lit on fire, and I floated on a spiritual cloud for quite a few months afterward. I haven't experienced anything quite like it since, although beats and rhythms of that tune do come back to me from time to time. It can be so tempting to chase spiritual fireworks, when in reality, they are merely the celebration or outpouring of months, days, or years of steady preparation. You need a firm surface to launch from and a steady foundation on which to build. Oftentimes, moments of great spiritual renewal come after a season of quiet faithfulness or because of the fervent prayers of someone on our behalf.

You have created a firm foundation here by showing up and putting in the work of processing your grief. You've built a solid house, and now it's time to sit on the back porch and take a moment to celebrate how far you've come. Maybe it's not a bright explosion of gunpowder, smoke, and lights but more like a single sparkler extended in the hand of a hopeful child. Either way, the spark has been lit inside you, glowing like a live coal for these last few months as you've read these pages.

It might feel strange to celebrate as a griever because it doesn't look like the traditional things we celebrate (graduations, births, and weddings). Yet even those celebrations are tinted with a form of grief, as oftentimes they signify a transition where we must say goodbye to the person we used to be. Why can't loss be tainted with joy too? I celebrated the first time I nonchalantly told some-one, "My mom died of cancer several years ago," and my heart rate didn't speed up. I celebrated the relief of an anniversary passing where I could remember more of the good memories than the painful ones. I celebrated my cheesy sense of humor coming back to greet me like an old friend. I celebrated the first Thanksgiving I made pumpkin pie that tasted *almost* as good as hers. Instead of chasing fireworks, I learned to tend the embers.

What is there to celebrate in the darkness? That the light of a single spark can still pierce the darkness. The God who said, "'Let there be light' and there was light" (Genesis 1:3 NIV) has never, nor will he ever, be extinguished. No matter how dark the night, or the tribulation of our souls, he shines brighter. Sometimes celebrating in the midst of dark skies can seem like a rebellious or ridiculous act. Yet it reminds us that God has overcome the darkness, and one day, we will celebrate with him face to face. What a fireworks show that will be!

Dear Jesus, I cannot wait until I get to celebrate the darkness being conquered by your light.

You are the light of all mankind, and your "light keeps shining in the dark, and darkness has never put it out" (John 1:5 CEV).

Shine bright in my darkness today.

You mourn with those who mourn, and celebrate with those who celebrate. Amen.

DAY 82

HOPE FOR SPRING AGAIN

For in this hope we were saved; but hope that is seen is no hope at all. Who hopes for what he can already see? But if we hope for what we do not yet see, we wait for it patiently.
—Romans 8:24–25 BSB

My neighbors planted bulbs in the winter that sprang up as bright yellow daffodils each spring. I would admire them from my window. Hope is like this in life: even though it may seem at times like a dark, grubby, mottled mess, when the time is right, it will bloom. Audrey Hepburn said, "To plant a garden is to believe in tomorrow," and the same thing can be said for hope. You can hope in the darkest of times and wait on the porch like I used to for the first signs of new life. Hope will always come through the darkness to search for the light.

I used to think that hope was just cheery optimism in a spiritual package. In reality, hope is unafraid to get down into the dark, muddy earth. Hope has grit and tenacity instead of sugar-coated lies. Hope often grows underneath the ground for a long time before anyone sees it. Hope grows within you when you begin to say to yourself, "Yes, I still ask why. Yes, I miss them like crazy. Yes, I am still sad. But my grief does not diminish God's goodness." God's promises to protect us, be with us, and strengthen us don't lose their luster, even when tragedy temporarily dims our eyes. Hope begins as the quiet wait of winter, until spring finally bursts forth.

The first spring after my mom died, my husband Jesse and I went for a walk around our neighborhood. Like a young child taking its first steps, my soul felt wobbly and unsteady in the starkness of spring's first rays. As we continued to stroll down the sidewalk, I realized that my sun-starved body needed vitamin D more than I had realized after a long winter of grieving. Along the sidewalk were bright clusters of yellow daffodils, turned toward the sky. Get outside today if you can and admire the trees and plants around you. Remind yourself they all started out as seeds in the ground. If you are able, you might even plant some seeds or bulbs yourself and dig your fingers into the soil. As you go about your day, you can say to Jesus, "Even if it's hard to hope again, I plant my hope in you. I trust you. I know that you will make it spring again." God will always grieve with us, and he will always hope for us.

Dear Lord, I do not place my hope in timelines, circumstances, or even the weather outside.

I plant the bulb of hope in my heart, grounded on your character and your promises.

You come through like spring always does each year.

I trust in you, even as I grieve.

I hope for what I cannot see, and I wait for it patiently. Amen.

DAY 83

LOVE IS ALWAYS WITH YOU

And I pray that you and all God's holy people will have the power to understand the greatness of Christ's love—how wide and how long and how high and how deep that love is.
—Ephesians 3:18 NCV

A few of my summers in college were spent working at a summer day camp for kids who had undergone difficult life circumstances and had emotional or behavioral issues. One of my campers was inquisitive, curious, and highly anxious. He could spend thirty minutes showing you grasshoppers outside with no sense of time or urgency. He also adamantly refused to leave the lake where we would swim without major intervention most days. One time, he kept screaming, "No!" as the counselors calmly repeated that it was time to go and we needed to head toward the bus. Finally, one of the directors walked into the water, fully clothed, and talked with the camper. He gently side-hugged the student and guided him back to the shore. All of the fight and struggle melted away from the camper, and he fell asleep on the bus ride home.

That day at the lake has stayed with me because it was such a healing moment in the midst of a very challenging summer. There were so many sweet moments, such as encouraging a camper to ride a horse for the first time and jump off the diving board at the pool. Yet there were also days of heartbreak, where a child would return to an unstable home, and we could do nothing to stop it. Two of my favorite campers hid one day in the bathrooms during check-in and went missing for a couple of hours. A policeman picked them up at a gas station just a short walk from the camp. I remember helping my other campers with an arts-and-crafts project later that day, trying to stay present. I kept cutting out paper hearts, and as I did, I felt like mine was being ripped in half for these two campers. They had experienced abandonment, death, rejection, and abuse. These experiences may have taught them that it was safer to run, even if it was away from people who cared about them. "Why can't I fix this for them?" I thought to myself. And then I realized that it wasn't my job to save or rescue anyone, and these kids weren't "projects," like little paper hearts for me to arrange the way I wanted to. I could wade into the deep waters with them, but it was up to them if they would come back out.

When Jesus met John the Baptist for the first time, he got in the water with him to be baptized. John had been performing baptisms, which meant immersing people in water as a picture of them being cleansed by God, before Jesus officially started his public ministry. John was confused because his role was to "prepare the way" for Jesus. He said to Jesus, "I need to be baptized by you, and do you come to me?" (Matthew 3:14 ESV). I love that Jesus wanted to be baptized by John. It shows a personal God who wants to come alongside people. When Jesus rose up from the water, God's Spirit descended upon him like a dove and said, "This is my Son, whom I love" (Matthew 3:17 NIV).

On my toughest days, when I'm floundering in the darkest waters of grief, I like to imagine that Jesus comes beside me and says, "This is my daughter, whom I love." My grief is not a project for him to fix, but an opportunity for his Spirit to descend from heaven to comfort me. Like my coworker that day at the lake, Jesus is not intimidated or overwhelmed by my situation. I can look to Jesus to be the calm and patient guide I need during the hardest parts of my life.

Dear Father, thank you for always working with me and not against me.

You enter the deepest waters and invite me to renew my spirit in your healing.

I pray that I would have a deeper understanding of your love.

I cannot wait to explore how wide and how long and how high and how deep that love is. Amen.

DAY 84

REMAIN LIGHT AS YOU FORGIVE OTHERS

Do not judge, and you will not be judged. Do not condemn, and you will not be condemned. Forgive, and you will be forgiven.
—Luke 6:37 NIV

"You've gained some weight. Don't get fat after I die, OK?" my mom said one day as she sat next to me on the couch. One of the hardest parts about my mom dying was that I couldn't resolve any conflict between us from her last days. Inside, I felt betrayed and mad. It wasn't just one isolated comment from her, but a pattern of thinly veiled criticisms when she was sick. When I made her oatmeal, I put one too many blueberries in it. When I leaned over her to adjust her pillow, she complained about my body odor. Any attempts to help her were met with eye rolls and sighs. Nothing I did was right because it really wasn't about me. She was in pain as a rapidly progressing disease took over her body. Sweet moments between us before she died felt few and far between. As she endured rounds of chemo and pain meds that altered her moods, the warm and protective mother I knew before turned distant and harsh. As she lost control, she tried to control the people around her.

Before my mom died, I treated forgiveness like a pack of saltines growing stale in the pantry—something I only had to use for emergencies or when I really felt sick but not necessary for daily use. Intellectually, I knew forgiveness was important, but it became intensely personal as I sorted through my grief. I was angry at my mom for not being able to give me the heartfelt goodbye I needed. I was angry at friends who didn't come to her memorial service. I was irritated at people who asked me, "What's God been teaching you lately?" because I had no easy answers for them. I was even mad at myself for being so angry. My anger lingered as I struggled to find the energy to process it.

The hurtful words my mom and others had said began to replay over and over again in my mind at 3 a.m. Justifying the reasons why my mom said what she did, or why my friends didn't show up, did not bring any relief. After a while, my energy began to return and I had the mental space to start processing. Holding onto the hurt my mom and friends had caused me was damaging not only to me but toward my relationship with God. Even though I couldn't talk things out with my mom, I began to talk it out with God.

As I began the process of forgiving my mom, I also began to remember the happier times too. I remembered how we used to dance to the end credits of her favorite movies. How she would pull my hair back when I ate soup, even when I was an adult. How she thought the world of us kids. My anger, which felt all-consuming, faded to a glowing ember. My anger helped alert me to my pain, but it prevented me from feeling and processing other emotions as well. Eventually, it became just another emotion alongside many others. Forgiveness felt like water to me in those days of early grief. Eventually, I needed it more than I needed my anger in order to thrive.

After talking to other grieving people, I've learned that anger is a common reaction to loss. If you've been hurt by the people around you while grieving, maybe you've experienced it too. If I could go back, I would tell myself that you don't have to forgive everyone and everything all at the same time. There just isn't enough energy left over to process all of it. God, however, is an endless resource for how to reconcile and forgive others. He is "slow to anger and abounding in steadfast love, forgiving iniquity and transgression" (Numbers 14:18 ESV). I don't have to figure it all out on my own because he's been forgiving humans since the beginning of time. Forgiveness doesn't lessen the hurt I feel; it just means I'm not responsible for resolving it on my own. I'm no longer waiting for an apology I can't get but looking forward to a reunion in God's presence.

Dear God, help me forgive others like you forgive me for the hurtful things I've said and done.

I'm tired of feeling angry all the time, and I'm ready to feel other emotions.

I need your forgiveness like water today to sustain and revive me. Amen.

DAY 85

REMAIN READY FOR HIGH ADVENTURE

You see me when I travel and when I rest at home. You know everything I do. You know what I am going to say even before I say it, Lord. *You go before me and follow me. You place your hand of blessing on my head.* —Psalm 139:3–5 NLT

Lowering down the roll-up door of our moving truck was the last step. It was time to go. We were not riding off into the sunset. Instead, we were driving off into a summer rainstorm. I was both terrified and excited. We were leaving behind Bellingham, Washington, for the town of Eugene, Oregon. Jesse was going to start an accelerated grad school program for chemistry, and I was going to try to write a book. I gripped the faux leather trim of the window of our car as I watched my father-in-law start up the U-Haul truck. "What awaited me in this new town? Why was it time to leave?" I thought to myself. I gave the glassy lake view, rippled with raindrops, one last glance and repeated to myself the line my dad had said to me the week before: "High adventure!" I turned my head and looked toward the slick road ahead of us, unsure of what was next.

High adventure usually refers to intense outdoor activities like rock climbing or hiking. Why not refer to the exciting new opportunities in our lives in the same way? For me, it's oftentimes helpful to reframe change and transitions as epic journeys with many highs and lows. Even if you don't find yourself on a mountaintop today, or taking in transcendent views below, you're embarking on a high adventure now. You are navigating uncharted lands of healing and rediscovering who you are. Faith, hope, and love remain your constant companions. You are going places that your loved one will never get to see in person, so let them experience it through your eyes. Narrate the new vistas, and let their memory come along. Acknowledge that you're journeying on with newfound faith, renewed hope, and deepening depths of love.

My first night spent in Eugene, I watched a colorful sunset from the back deck of our new apartment. The air was warm and balmy as I looked out across the outdoor pool directly across from us. Jesse and I shared salty slices of pizza after we unloaded the U-Haul, and we talked about how the trees looked different here. Two weeks later, I would make my first friend. The next summer, I would go to my first writer's conference. We would face infertility, a pandemic, and the five-year anniversary of my mom's death. This is where we would buy our first home and get our miracle baby. Jesse would get a job working as a chemist developing resins for plywood products. My sister and her family would unexpectedly join us here in this town several years later. So much adventure awaited me, but it all remained unknown as I stood in my apartment that day, surrounded by unpacked boxes.

Jesus calls us to high adventure with him. To take in the new views of his love and explore the highest highs and the deepest lows where he will always go with us. We don't need to go to a new place to experience a refresh of his presence. He meets us on the rain-soaked roads of our future, slick with danger. He rides beside us as we take in new views and ask ourselves, "Who am I without them—in these places they've never seen?" He goes before, behind, and ahead of us. For him, this is not new, but rather the intersection of meeting each other over and over again. There's no tidy bow to bring resolution to our lives, but there is the invitation to continue the adventure of discovering who God is. Are you in?

Dear Jesus, help me reframe the unknown events ahead of me as an adventure, with you as my guide: "You go before me and follow me" (Psalm 139:5 NIV).

I'm surrounded on all sides by you.

I love you Lord, not because things have always gone my way, but because you have always gone with me along the way. Amen.

DAY 86

FAITH'S ETERNAL RAYS

Fight the good fight of the faith. Take hold of the eternal life to which you were called when you made your good confession in the presence of many witnesses. —1 Timothy 6:12 NIV

What does eternity mean to you?" my small group leader asked me. I was twelve years old, sitting in the dry grass next to a bluff, overlooking the waters below. We were having small group time during middle school summer camp, and I felt like my whole perspective on life was changing. Between games of capture the flag and swimming in the ocean, our guest speaker talked about eternity and how we could live our lives in response to it. As I looked out at the yellow sun dancing on the horizon of the water below, I realized that I had never thought about eternity in relation to myself. Jesus would endure forever, but what did that have to do with me? "I don't know what eternity is, but I want it," I blurted out to my leader, saying the first thing that came to my mind.

"Why do you want eternity if you don't know the Jesus you'll be spending forever with?" I wondered to myself afterward. Eternity, before that moment, had been an abstract concept I was comfortable leaving to the adults to figure out. I wanted to go to heaven because that's what Sunday school had taught me. Quietly, something shifted in me that day. I had no idea where to start, but I wanted to try to get to know Jesus. Like the sunset that day dipping beneath the horizon, my childhood ideas of who God is were setting. They were being replaced with a hunger for answers and a curiosity about God. Little did I know that I would be wrestling with big questions about life and death very soon.

The following fall, a boy from our youth group died instantly, along with his mom and baby sister, when they crashed headfirst into a garbage truck. His name was Taylor, and he had made a recommitment to God at that same summer camp. This loss devastated our entire church, and me and my fellow middle schoolers had no idea how to process our grief. I couldn't help but wonder: "Why did he die? Why him and not me?" I pulled out my velvet diary from elementary school, and I began to furiously write my questions. When my handwriting couldn't keep up, I began typing page after page. I couldn't stop talking to God. I didn't understand why Taylor and his family died, but I knew that his convictions at fourteen years old mattered. That meant that my commitment to God at twelve years old could mean something too.

That first experience with grief opened up a conversation between me and Jesus. More than ten years later, when my mom died, I remembered the middle schooler I was back then—hungry for answers and full of questions. I needed to talk to him honestly and openly again. It doesn't matter what age I am, or what is going on in my life, Jesus still asks me this question: "Do you want to spend eternity with me?" The answer, for me, is an unequivocal yes. There's still so much I don't have figured out about life. I have just as much, if not more, questions for God now than I did as a child. All I know is that God has remained steady in his pursuit of me.

Even if I drift away from him, I know that his love waits for me. It's never too early or too late for me to start talking to him. The thief next to Jesus on the cross exemplifies this. Two thieves were dying next to Jesus. One hurled insults at him, and the other defended him, saying, "We are punished justly, getting what we deserve. ... But this man has done nothing wrong." The thief then makes a bold request, asking Jesus to remember him after he dies. Jesus tells him, "I tell you the truth, today you will be with me in paradise" (Luke 23:41, 43 NCV). The dying thief's faith *mattered* to Jesus. Jesus used up some of his last few breaths on earth to promise him eternity. We all matter to Jesus. It's never too late, and it's never too early, to start talking to him again.

Dear Jesus, there is still so much I don't understand.

Why do some people die at such a young age?

How can I even begin to comprehend eternity when my life is so short?

Even if I don't get answers to my questions, I'm going to keep asking.

Thank you for being a God who cares about middle schoolers, dying thieves, and grieving people.

It's never too late for me to reach out to you. Amen.

DAY 87

HOPE'S ETERNAL CERTAINTY

Yet, O Lord, you are our Father; we are the clay,
and you are our potter; we are all the work of your hand.
—Isaiah 64:8 NRSV

This grief journey is predictable in its unpredictability, and I'm sure you have begun to recognize its winding path within your own life. As I approached the final stretch of writing these words, my beloved counselor of four years unexpectedly died from cancer, and it would be an understatement to say that she was a great cheerleader of my work. She was *so* excited to share it with her other clients when it came to fruition. I also lost my beloved grandpa, or Papa, at the start of this writing process. Papa died the day after I gave birth to my son, Lukas. As I embraced the newness of tending and caring for my own child, I also grieved the loss of these spiritual elders in my life. If you were to wring out the pages of this book, I would not be surprised if my own tears spilled out of it. These pages are drenched with many kinds of grief.

Like that saying from my dad that I mentioned at the beginning of this book, our souls are truly precious seeds encased in fragile shells, like walnuts scattered on the ground underneath a tree. We grow and tend, break and mend. I needed a refresher course in how to grieve in light of faith, hope, and love. I probably will need one again in the future. At the beginning of this book, I wrote: "Jesus stands with us as a seed of hope planted within our souls," which reminded me that, even as I healed from fresh grief wounds, hope was always there. The Katrina who wanted to run from the hospital with a sick mom needed to hear these words just as much as the Katrina in the childbirth recovery room of the maternity wing hearing her Papa had died in the first light of morning.

When I told people that I was writing a grief devotional, some people said, "That must be so healing," and I was surprised by how true their conclusion was. The story of my grief seemed like a pile of messy clay before I sat down and started to mold it. Before writing this book, I remembered it as a time where I felt disconnected from friends, endured insomnia and migraines, and my emotions were all over the place. And I still think that's true. When I took the time to reflect back, I began to see what I couldn't see then. I could see the imprints of God's thumb and fingers, molding the muddy clay as it spun in circles. He formed in me a hope I could always come back to, glazed and shining like a ceramic mug on the shelf waiting for coffee.

I wish I could tell you that this will be your only experience with grief. But from my own experience, people enter this world and leave it every day. My counselor, Alicia, immigrated from Trinidad when she was a young mom and had to make a life for her family in an entirely new country. She told me often, in her calming Caribbean accent, "Make a note of this. So when this happens again, you can come back to this truth." So today, make a note of this: hope endures. Write it down on paper, and tape it to your bathroom mirror or inside the cupboard where you store your coffee grounds. Jesus became mortal to create immortality for us clay people. We are broken, fragile, and commonplace and yet moldable and valuable in God's hands. And that hope is something we can always count on and return to in this unpredictable life.

Dear God, let me be a walking, talking,
and breathing example of what it looks like
to hope, even when things are messy
and unexpected.

Help me to lay down my life before you in the big
and little ways. Amen.

DAY 88

LOVE'S ETERNAL ADVOCATE

But when the Father sends the Advocate as my representative—that is, the Holy Spirit—he will teach you everything and will remind you of everything I have told you. —John 14:26

My favorite part of the opening shift at the dessert shop was stirring the large tub of buttercream because it smelled like vanilla ice cream. Before the open sign was turned on outside, it was my job to frost a couple dozen cupcakes for the display case. Soon, the demand for cupcakes grew so large that it was no longer feasible for me to frost them all. I missed the quiet ritual of prepping and piping the icing before the shop grew busy and loud. I didn't, however, miss the stress of transferring them to the display case as people lined up outside the door, worried I would drop one or run out of time. With one less task to complete, I found myself more present as I unlocked the door and waved the first people inside. I've never been a fan of any kind of change, whether little or big. I have always struggled to let go, whether it's a small change involving cupcakes, or a bigger change like my grief entering a new stage.

When I hit the four-year anniversary of my mother's death, I realized that my grief was changing. Initially, I was resistant to this change because I wanted my grief to stay static and, in my mind, more controllable. God, through the Holy Spirit, was teaching me how to set down emotional burdens I didn't need to carry anymore. I began to let go of the bitterness that my mom was sick at my wedding. I could finally say, "I'm so happy she was there." I couldn't say that for the longest time because I didn't know how to sit with my feelings of anger and thankfulness at the same time. Another sign my grief was changing: I could tell my mom's story without feeling panicky or tearing up. Those feelings and reactions were all valid and normal, but God wanted me to make space for other emotions too. That year was intense and involved lots of journaling to God, talks with my therapist, and long walks with friends. Finally, I began to feel lighter. My grief was not "done"; it was just different now.

Perhaps your grief is starting to change too. Maybe it's time to ask the Holy Spirit: "What can I let go of today?" Then, talk with a trusted friend or counselor in your life and begin making space for all of your emotions. I found this part of my grief painful and difficult to talk about but, nevertheless, a skill God was honing in my life. Current peace doesn't mean I don't still have questions, doubts, or miss my mom any less. Peace means that God highlights aspects of his character and how they can be incorporated into my grief. Whether you are more apt to embrace or resist change, I hope you recognize God's gentle nudges reminding you of his wisdom today.

I'm no longer carrying every part of my grief in my own two hands, constantly worried that I will drop something and make a mess. Sometimes, a mess is required in order to acknowledge how much I need God to help me out. I still don't like change, but I recognize now that sometimes it is for the best. Our grief will continue to change, with both heavier and lighter days as we go about my lives. What doesn't ever change is that God's guidance is given freely to us, and we don't have to be afraid of what comes next.

Dear Jesus, instead of balancing my grief on my own strength, I surrender it to you.

You have given your Holy Spirit to guide me in your ways of love and peace.

You remind me that your love follows me through all of the changes of life.

Thank you for creating something new and different within me. Amen.

DAY 89

REMAIN ETERNAL

Then Samuel took a stone and set it up between Mizpah and Shen and called its name Ebenezer; for he said, "Till now the Lord has helped us." —1 Samuel 7:12 ESV

In the three years leading up to my mom's diagnosis, I collected rocks on my windowsill. I would pick out a rock from the beach each summer and write on it a theme that I noticed God was highlighting in my life. They were inspired by the Ebenezer stone in the Bible that Samuel set up to remember the things God had done. On the first rock, I wrote "Hope" because of the sign at the cancer fundraiser, and the name of the summer camp I worked at was called "Ray of Hope." The second year, I wrote "Faith" because of learning how to have faith like a tree, embracing my own spiritual maturity, and admiring the grit of the women in my family. The third rock was "Love," which represented learning how to accept God's love and the beginning of my relationship with Jesse. One day, I read 1 Corinthians 13:13 and realized that the last three years of my life were perfectly encapsulated in this one, powerful verse: "Now these three remain: faith, hope, and love. But the greatest of these is love."

I held these rocks in my palm and thought how my life was coming together in such a tidy way. Then my mom got sick. Life became anything but tidy, and he was not done with me yet. These three simple stones represented the times God had been faithful and loving to me in the past, and I now had a choice whether I would trust him with my future. I needed God's faith, hope, and love more than ever.

Several years after my mom died, my friend Kamille taught a storytelling class at my church that focused on honing your own story so you could share it with others. The turnout was initially disappointing, with only three of us showing up, including her husband. I laugh now at the symbolism of three people showing up to a class where I laid down the bones of a book built upon three strong, central themes: faith, hope, and love. I saw hope represented in the bubbly enthusiasm of the young woman sitting next to me, ready to embark on the next chapter of her life. I saw a deep faith in the steady support of my friend's thoughtful and analytical husband. And finally, love, in the passion I had to help people who were grieving. We were three people with three unique stories.

Near the end of the class, Kamille gave the three of us a bubble map to start brainstorming our stories. As I stared down at the paper, I thought of the three rocks I had set on my windowsill, worn smooth by saltwater. I made three large bubbles in the middle and wrote: "Faith, Hope, and Love," and then I chose several stories for each of these big themes. Written on the paper before me was the skeletal structure for these ideas to start walking, breathing, and talking. It wasn't a neat or tidy story, but the themes were starting to come to life.

Today, take a few rocks and several sheets of paper. Write down the words "faith," "hope," and "love" on each rock. Branching out of these three themes, list one or two examples from your life where God has shown you these truths on the pieces of paper. Grief can show up at any time, often without warning, and it's helpful to have something physical to remind you of who God is in the moment. I think there's a good reason Samuel chose something permanent and stable like a rock to remind him of what God had done. I hope that the truths of who God is are not just written on rocks but written on your heart. God is not done with you, and you will need faith, hope, and love every day of your life.

Dear God, I need reminders of your faith, hope,
and love in my life.

You are stable, permanent, and faithful even when
things feel chaotic and untidy.

You have come with me this far and will continue
with me as I go forward. Amen.

DAY 90

THESE THREE REMAIN

And now these three remain: faith, hope and love.
But the greatest of these is love. —1 Corinthians 13:13 NIV

My friend Allisyn met me for coffee six years ago and surprised me with the thoughtful gift of a ceramic mug with a typewriter etched on the side. We both shared a passion for writing and books, and her gift reminded me of that. She told me confidently, "I think you should write a book," and that cold December day, over a spicy Mexican mocha, a dream within me was reopened. A dream my mom never got to see, brought to fruition in my life. Yet I like to imagine that she's bragging to whatever angel or saint she's currently surrounded by and can't stop talking about it.

I hope that, as you finish this book, you too find dreams within you reopened. Perhaps one that the Holy Spirit has given you a while ago, and all you need is some encouragement to pursue it. Grief is a continual part of our lives as people who have experienced the death of a loved one. But grief does not get the final say in our lives because God's faith, hope, and love continue beyond anything we experience in this life. I hope you can recognize the growth in your own life as you've read through this book. God's faith, hope, and love are always a welcome gift, waiting for you to open when you need them most.

Today, I'm sitting at my desk, trying to write these last few words. I keep watching the apple tree sway in the light autumn breeze, glancing occasionally at the baby monitor to make sure my son is still napping. My sister just texted me and my brother a photo of a T-shirt that says, "My mom died and all I got was this free T-shirt," and asked, "Is this joke too dark?" I'm chuckling at how humor can often be found in the darkest places. My dad is beginning to date again, and it's both exciting and strange to give him dating advice. I'm tempted to procrastinate writing these last few sentences by looking up therapists available in my area, since Jesse asked me last night, "Have you thought about finding a new counselor?" This is grief eight years later. I can see her face in my mind clear as day right now, and I remember her embarrassing dance moves and the way she put cinnamon in every baked good. Her presence is close and dynamic as I can sense the pride she has for me in pursuing this dream of writing a book.

We remain here, without our person, and God remains with us as we wait for the full resolution to our pain. He remains, even when we've lost someone close to us. He remains, even as we experience grief again in our lives. He remains until the day we cross the finish line into heaven, arms held high in victory. He remains the source of all life and love—today, yesterday, and for eternity. Faith, hope, and love remain, but the greatest of these—the one we can spend our whole lives adventuring toward—is God's love.

I would like to leave you with a prayer from Numbers 6:24–26 (NKJV):

> The LORD bless you and keep you;
> The LORD make His face shine upon you,
> And be gracious to you;
> The LORD lift up His countenance upon you,
> And give you peace.

SCRIPTURE QUOTATIONS

Scripture quotations marked (MSG) are from THE MESSAGE. Copyright © by Eugene H. Peterson 1993, 1994, 1995, 1996, 2000, 2001, 2002. Used by permission of Tyndale House Publishers, Inc.

Scripture quotations marked (NCV) are from The Holy Bible, New Century Version®. Copyright © 2005 by Thomas Nelson, Inc.

Scripture quotations marked (NKJV) are from the New King James Version. Copyright 1982 by Thomas Nelson. Used by permission. All rights reserved.

Scripture quotations marked (NRSV) are from the New Revised Standard Version Bible, copyright © 1989, National Council of the Churches of Christ in the United States of America. Used by permission. All rights reserved.